Behind the Masks

Behind the Masks
Personality Disorders
in Religious Behavior

Wayne E. Oates

The Westminster Press
Louisville, Kentucky 40202

Book design by Gene Harris

First edition

Published by The Westminster Press®
Louisville, Kentucky 40202

PRINTED IN THE UNITED STATES OF AMERICA

9 8 7 6 5 4

Library of Congress Cataloging-in-Publication Data

Oates, Wayne Edward, 1917–
  Behind the masks.

  Bibliography p.
  1. Pastoral psychology. 2. Personality, Disorders of
—Religious aspects—Christianity. I. Title.
BV4012.O19 1987   253.5   87-8221
ISBN 0-664-24028-3 (pbk.)

To
Swan Haworth, Ph.D.
My fellow
Christian pastor

Contents

Acknowledgments

Authorities on personality disorders agree that literature on the topic is very scarce. The early work of Hervey Cleckley, *The Mask of Sanity* (first published in 1941), stood as a major source for years. I have profited greatly by this book, as I acknowledge by my title. The extensive work of the Task Force of the American Psychiatric Association chaired by Robert L. Spitzer, in the descriptions set forth in the *Diagnostic and Statistical Manual of Mental Disorders,* third edition, 1980 (DSM III), has been a definitive guideline for my work. Theodore Millon's critical and historical study *Disorders of Personality: DSM III; Axis II* has been indispensable to me and to my students in our intensive seminar, case history, theoretical understanding, and group self-searches on the eleven categories of personality disorders. His work is cited often in this book because he has thought more, said more, and embraced more of the wisdom of a century or two of other people's work than anyone else I can find.

My search, however, has concentrated on the treasures of biblical and historical Christian experience of this large spectrum of human suffering and stubbornness of mind. My central concern has been with the purposes and functions of the church and its ministry in relation to the people behind the masks in their day-to-day ways of living and working with each other. Consequently, the wisdom literature of the scriptures and the writings of persons such as John Bunyan and William Shakespeare have been primary sources, and the teachings of Jesus and of Paul have been searchlights of understanding and empathy.

I am especially indebted to my colleagues in the Department of Psychiatry and Behavioral Sciences of the University of Louisville School of Medicine. For over twelve years we have worked together in clinics, case conferences, and grand rounds, in reciprocal referral of persons in dire straits, and in profound personal friendships. Footnotes cannot express my gratitude to them; each page of this book reflects their presence and wisdom in my life.

I especially acknowledge the inspiration and participation of my colleagues Henlee Barnette, James Hyde, Drexel Rayford, Bettye Howell, and Katherine Thornton Williams; they are "persons for all seasons" with whom I have shared breakthroughs with difficult patients. We have, in unison, asked of the Lord, "Lord, why could we not heal this one?" Yet we have a common commitment: "To heal some, to remedy others, and to care always."

None of this book would be in manuscript form at all without the exceptional competence and word-processing skills of Cindy Meredith of the Office Services of The Southern Baptist Theological Seminary. She has ministered to us all in her dedicated skills. To her I express my deep gratitude.

Prologue

You and I like our relationships with others to go smoothly and in an orderly fashion. We can tolerate disorder up to a certain point. Beyond that, people who live in a recurrent or perpetual state of disorder irritate, aggravate, and frustrate us. They wear on our nerves. They enrage or depress us or alternately do both. We overtake them in first one fault and then another. Our Christian conscience disturbs us because we find something of ourselves in such persons. We go to our prayers and examine our own selves, so that we may not be tempted to live as they do in order to fight fire with fire. They move from one crisis to another, though, and this cycle repeats itself. No amount of "helping" them seems to have any lasting effect. As we look around and see how these persons relate to other people, we see that we are not alone. They relate to others even as they do to us.

The most stress comes to us, the most wear and tear of life is ours, when persons with these troublesome ways of life are members of our own families. We, like the Israelites at Jericho, must go round and round the walls they erect, blowing our horns. Unlike Joshua and his troops, we never manage to bring the walls down. Yet these persons are our own kin, often a father, a mother, a brother, a sister, a son, a daughter. On sleepless nights we may search our own histories and find—in our self-recriminations—a dozen things we ourselves have done that may have "caused" this loved one to be as he or she is. This is often the topic of pillow talk between mothers and fathers of a son or daughter who is in and out of a job, in and out of a marriage, in and out of the drug scene, or constantly playing Uproar at a family gathering. Often it is the topic of conversation between high-achieving siblings of a ne'er-do-well brother or sister. Or it may be just the reverse. One

brother or sister may be such a smooth operator that he or
she wheels and deals into much money and symbols of afflu-
ence while the rest of the "good" brothers and sisters go to
church, work at ordinary jobs, and barely manage to keep the
bills paid. Less often, there may be an uncle who is a skinflint.
He gathers where he did not sow. He picks up where he did
not put anything down. He won't share his goods with his own
children, much less with those of his brothers and sisters. Or
for another kinsperson the family members have to toe the
line, stand up straight, and watch every move they make. If
this is a man, he becomes alarmed when the laundry leaves a
slight wrinkle in his shirt cuff. Or, if this is a woman, every
speck of dust is immediately destroyed by her obsessive clean-
liness, and each piece of tableware must be exactly half an
inch apart from the others.

What gets us, though, is finding these disorders of everyday
life in the conduct of fellow church members. We are alternately alarmed or sweet-talked and enchanted by them if they
are pastors, ministers of music, ministers of education, ministers of youth, or prominent lay leaders in the church. In these
instances, such persons' outlandish behaviors become the
topic of many telephone conversations between church members. They are the favorite subject of rumors generated in the
imaginations of people who otherwise would have little to talk
about and even less to think about. In this sense, persons with
such ways of life thrive on the boredom of other people.

How you and I can understand and relate constructively to
such people is my concern in the pages of this book. These
ordinarily are sane people, but they wear their sanity as a
mask, not as the outward expression of an inward possession.
They are religious, but we are mystified that neither the sacraments of the liturgical churches nor the ordinances and
"professions of faith" of the churches of the revival traditions
have changed their obstinate ways of life, but have only
glossed them over with a veneer of religiosity.

"Ways of life" is what they are. The King James Version of
the Bible speaks of "conversation," which means a person's
pattern of conduct, his or her "walk." When you and I read
our Bibles closely, we find vivid portraits of people who lived
like this—in the parables of Jesus and in the Old and New
Testament descriptions of character disorders in biblical personalities. The wisdom literature of the book of Proverbs and
the Psalms is replete with appraisals and approaches to such
behavior. The writings of the early church fathers in hand-
books of confession such as John Cassian's *Institutes* reflect

profound awareness of disordered behaviors in religious persons. John Bunyan's *Pilgrim's Progress* portrays not only such character disorders but attitudes and ways of dealing with them within our awareness of the presence of God.

Until recently, psychiatrists, psychologists, and specially trained pastoral counselors have lumped together all these difficult persons or put them into a very few categories. Usually they have responded to persons with such habitual patterns of life in much the same way that laypersons do—emotionally and impatiently. Early on, these patients were called psychopaths. Then some discrimination was attempted and several diagnostic terms were employed: "sociopath," "inadequate personality," "hysterical personality." More often such persons were grouped again under one poorly defined but vehemently expressed classification, that of "character disorders." Disgust, humor, and derision ripple through psychiatric case conferences less often now than happened earlier. The therapeutic community of a psychiatric unit becomes a surrogate family to patients. As a result, that community quickly becomes the next group which people with personality disorders treat as they do their biological family, their employers, and their spouses and children.

Since the Vietnam War, generally speaking, and more specifically since 1980, the American Psychiatric Association has formed a very careful description of eleven different patterns of personality disorders. They are sufficiently different to be distinguished from each other, yet they have enough in common to exist in a spectrum of life-styles that tend to blur into each other. Consequently they are not hard-and-fast entities, like apples and oranges, but are like fluid and intermingling colors in a collage of light. They are lifelong personality patterns that people carry with them through whatever illness they may develop. Understanding these life patterns can provide a context of wisdom for appreciating and treating the lifelong personal way of life of individuals, just as the more florid symptoms they present in the crisis of hospitalization are treated. As I heard the eminent psychoanalyst Franz Alexander say to a seminar in which I was a member, "The more we study and treat the acute illnesses of people, the more we cease to be mere physicians and the more we take on the functions of teacher, clergyperson, and parent guiding and encouraging the persons in their way of life."

A widely read author who has dealt extensively with persons enmeshed in these maladaptive ways of life is Hervey Cleckley. In his book *The Mask of Sanity,* one main contention is that their personality disorders are semblances of sanity but not an authentic way of life. In the course of living ways have developed that are not genuine, ways that appear to be basically human without actually being so. Hence, his title "the mask of sanity." You and I will be concerned in the following pages with humanely, gently, but persistently unmasking these ways of life. Such persons have a pseudo self overlying the image of God in them. Our prayer in relation to each one of these masking life-styles is that we may enable the real persons to emerge. Then they can achieve the goal for which Socrates prayed: "O Lord, give me beauty in the inner being, and may the outward person and the inward person be at one."

The present-day psychiatric community have published their classification of personality disorders in the *Diagnostic and Statistical Manual of Mental Disorders,* third edition, or DSM III. This book has been in use since 1980. One member of the task force of physicians was Theodore Millon, an internationally known authority on the understanding and treatment of these ways of life, who has written a definitive text on the subject entitled *Disorders of Personality: DSM III; Axis II.* The elevenfold system of assessment followed in these texts uses different names, as follows:

DSM III	THEODORE MILLON
Dependent Personality	Submissive Pattern
Histrionic Personality	Gregarious Pattern
Narcissistic Personality	Egotistical Pattern
Antisocial Personality	Aggressive Pattern
Compulsive Personality	Conforming Pattern
Passive-Aggressive Personality	Negativistic Pattern
Schizoid Personality	Asocial Pattern
Avoidant Personality	Withdrawn Pattern
Borderline Personality	Unstable Pattern
Paranoid Personality	Suspicious Pattern
Schizotypal Personality	Eccentric Pattern

The original terms are forbidding, but Millon's renaming of them provides more linkage with the language and experience of our everyday life. One of my objectives is to speak of these walks of life, these ways of life, these patternings of personality in graphic everyday language that I myself can understand and that you and I can use in daily living. I want to do everything I can to demystify the wisdom of the behavioral sciences using my native Anglo-Saxon tongue and to do so with metaphor, story, and word pictures. That Millon helps in this process is evident, for example, when he speaks of the borderline personality as the "stably unstable" and the paranoid personality as "suspicious."

My chosen audience is not a group of fellow professors or a group of research persons in clinics, although I cherish their criticisms and colleagueship in the trenches where we work together daily. My chosen audience is the parent, the teacher, the student in college and seminary classes, and the Christian pastor. I address you directly in the second person so that I will be more likely to put myself in your place and speak to you emphatically and not in a detached manner. The distinctly religious expressions of these behaviors will be my central concern. Therefore, I hope this book can become a catalyst for group discussion between pastors and church members. I am persuaded that many times of tension in the life of the church family will be defused by more understanding and less name-calling, which downgrades and does violence to the persons of fellow Christians.

I

The Mask
of Dependence

A newborn human baby is one of the most helpless in creation, a quite unfinished being. Human infants are dependent upon others, usually parents, much longer than animal infants. This lengthened period of infancy calls for parental nurturance in decreasing abundance and intensity over a period of eighteen years. If the family has a tradition of college education, dependency may well extend into the twenty-fourth year.

Some parents and their children have a life-style of increasing doses of independence and responsibility for the growing child, adolescent, and young adult. Their goal is to provide an affectionate learning atmosphere in which children learn to stand on their own. As is taught by Jesus, children learn from parents to let go of the wonder of childhood and to leave father and mother in such a way as to honor them and not bring on them shame, embarrassment, and the feeling of having been failures as parents. This becomes one of the crucial tests of the wisdom of parents and the courage, self-definition, and self-reliance of sons and daughters.

There is a time to be dependent, and there is a time to be independent. One veteran pediatric nurse said, "Good parenting means not doing things for children that they can do for themselves and letting them experiment with doing things that won't hurt them, that they *think* they can do for themselves." This is difficult for the parent or teacher who repeatedly thinks, I would rather do something myself than watch them make a mess of it and never get around to doing it. Difficulty awaits the authoritarian parent, teacher, or pastor who issues orders and makes people do as they are told without any back talk. To be self-reliant is nearly impossible in a religious group, cult, sect, denomination, or hierarchy where masses of very dependent people follow every jot and tittle of what the religious dictator says. Such absolute authority may be appropriate in military combat when a soldier's life may depend upon the commands of the officer, or in an operating room where the surgeon has the incision open and the patient's life depends upon the staff doing as they are told. But these are survival situations of great intensity. They are not fit models for the daily living and learning of a family, a school, or a church over the long pull.

Failures of human nature in parenting, teaching, and vocational settings all produce people who, after the age of eighteen or twenty, are still as dependent as they were at three, four, or five.

Characteristics of the Dependent Way of Life

A portrait of those who exhibit the dependent way of life is somewhat as follows: These persons are generally likable, friendly, and obliging. In fact they may be so submissive to anything you say to them that you get the feeling they are overdoing it. They seem ready to be your slave! You become uncomfortable, unless you yourself have a strong need for slaves and want to clone yourself, and if you were that sort of person you would not be reading this book. More probably, you are like me. I have a strong need to help and am an inveterate care giver. An indiscriminate mothering impulse runs through many men and many more women. The dependent person seems so "helpless" we are caught in this tender trap.

On closer acquaintance with persons with a dependent way of life, you discover that they do not get strong directions for living from their own judgment and decision-making. As Erich Fromm says in *Man for Himself,* they feel that the source of all good is outside themselves and that the only way to get what they want—"be it material things, be it affection, love, knowledge, pleasure, is to receive it from that outside source" (Fromm 1947: 65–67). Fromm wrote the book with fresh memories of the dependent "escape from freedom" of a whole people in the Third Reich. Dependent upon the external authority of Hitler, a whole nation was caught up in a pathological, idolatrous dependency. (Fromm also describes several other personality life-styles to which we will be referring later. The serious student will be inspired by the authentic wisdom in this book.)

Another prominent characteristic of dependent persons is their perception of themselves as weak, fragile, and ineffectual. Such persons lack confidence in their own judgments and belittle their competencies and aptitudes. Do they perceive themselves as being made in the image of God, as persons for whom Christ died, as having unique gifts that are native endowments and "capital" for investing in life on their own? They do not. Such good news of the gospel of Christ falls as strange fire on strange altars. They grovel at the shrine of old oracles that have underrated them, considered them weak and inadequate and never going to amount to anything. Along with this low self-worth, they seethe in anxiety and indecision when faced with the responsibilities of school, employment, and marriage. They are constantly casting themselves on the mercy of people whom they perceive as superior to themselves.

The way of life of dependent persons is deficient in personal initiative and follow-through on tasks. You have difficulty forming a two-way working alliance with them, no matter what your role in their life is. If you are a parent, dependent sons or daughters expect you to indulge them with money, housing, and food no matter how many jobs they fail to get or keep. If you are a co-worker, such persons are the chronic flunkies who wait for someone to tell them what to do. They do what they are told and no more. Yet it is difficult to be too critical, because every person carrying a great deal of responsibility is grateful to have a "gofer," even though it is to the detriment of that person's long-term well-being. Initiative is missing in these persons. They abdicate responsibility.

Yet another characteristic of dependent persons is a docile, noncompetitive, and placid temperament. They stay out of social tension and interpersonal conflicts. They are laid back. If the person is a husband or wife, the resolution of growth crises of expanding the family budget, keeping close account of the income and expenditures, preparing meals and cleaning of the house, nurturing and caring for children are all left to the other mate. Some Christian interpretations of a wife's submission to her husband, and some secular "macho" stances, really gloss over a fundamentally dependent personality life-style in the man. *He* is placid; *she* worries too much and nags too much. She gets the uneasy feeling that she is more his mother substitute who is supposed to indulge his every need than a partner who shares responsibilities with him as a joint heir of the grace of life in Christ. On balance, the dependent spouse's peacefulness turns out to be inconsiderateness. Before God this person's prayers are hindered (1 Peter 3:7).

We can turn this coin of marriage over and see how the dependent wife is the one who is either submissive to such an extent that the Proverbs portrait of a wife who is more precious than jewels is never realized. She is her husband's weak, helpless worshiper at his throne. He is authoritarian and yet places the "little woman" on a pedestal. He earns all the money, pays all the bills, makes all the decisions; never teaches her (or permits her, if she already knows how) to balance the checkbook; never lets her know the cost of the operation of the home, the amount of money in the bank account, how to make large purchases such as a new house, a new car, or an adequate insurance and retirement program. He does not want her to worry "her pretty little head" over these mundane things. He is a gentle, benevolent tyrant. She is a dependent cream puff.

Yet if something happened to him—if he was called away to war, became seriously disabled by a stroke, or died—she would not know what to do or where to turn. She would become a "wailing widow."

Another characteristic of the dependent way of life is a superficial affability and good-naturedness. Dependent persons are just too sweet and nice to be real. Their Pollyanna outlook on life glosses over their own blunders. It minimizes the shortcomings of other people with a saccharine spirit that perplexes anyone listening to them. They disparage themselves while making excuses for injustices heaped upon them by others. The transparent denial in the syrupy sweetness of their very speech pattern is a noticeable trait.

A final characteristic of dependent persons is their isolation and fear of being alone. They hold on to and cling to their superiors at work. Their marriages are held on to even in the face of abuse, infidelity, and abandonment. Yet, as Millon says (1981:114), they have "learned the 'inferior' role well." Because of the way they play their role their partner gains a feeling of being "useful, sympathetic, stronger and competent." Note that those are the traits that dependent persons seek in their mates. I might add that dependent persons seek these same qualities in teachers, pastors, personal friends, and therapists!

Major Hazards of the Dependent Way of Life

Major hazards lie in wait for the dependent person. When these hazards hit them, they respond with intense behavior that often takes a religious form and content.

Separation Anxiety and Panic Attacks

Dependent persons are highly vulnerable to perceived, threatened, or actual separation from the persons upon whom they are addictively dependent. When separation actually happens, they are as often as not thrown into a panic.

For example, dependency panic shows up vividly in military basic training units, in the freshman class of colleges, in the new bride or bridegroom (possibly the one and possibly the other). These panic states are seen most often in persons from the ages of eighteen to twenty-five.

In American culture of the middle and upper classes, all of the above-named experiences call for persons to "leave father, mother, brother, sister," and all the familiar surroundings of home. Security-giving rituals of their family hearth are no longer a part of their day. A whole new set of rituals of the military, the college, or the newlyweds' home have to be learned and put in place. We commonly think of this anxiety as "homesickness" or nostalgia. To some extent many if not most people suffer these feelings. However, in dependent persons the separation anxiety overwhelms them and throws them into a panic, a terror inspired by a trifling cause or a misapprehension of danger. The word "panic" comes from Greek mythology. Pan was the god of the flocks and herds, and the patron deity of shepherds, hunters, and fishermen. When a herd stampeded, it was Pan who had caused their fear. A panic is the stampeding of the normal processes of rational thinking.

This overpowering fear arises from dependent persons' withdrawal from those who have filled their needs for outside support, nurturance, and emotional "supplies." Another factor in this withdrawal is the person's having to face up to adult responsibilities: doing schoolwork, mastering military discipline, supporting the needs of wife or husband. The panic itself is contagious and prompts others to be solicitous and nurturant and to relieve the dependent person of responsibility.

The religious expression of panic takes several forms. One

person may latch on feverishly to a close-knit religious group or a strong, all-promising religious leader. You can supply the names of groups that are personality cults built around the dictums, rituals, rules, regulations, and sayings of one man or woman. Dependent devotees are enamored of the "seductions of the spirit" set forth by this person. The group-think of the many other followers massively reinforces the dependency, lack of responsibility, and escape from freedom that this kind of religious captivity provides the compliant soul of the dependent personality.

Other dependent persons will be far more isolated and less gregarious. They will express thoughts such as these to a close friend, chaplain, college or seminary professor, or pastor of the church they attend: "I find that I cannot get any answers to my prayers. God does not seem to be there for me any more." "I am afraid that in leaving home I went against God's will. If I am to be in his will, I think I must go back home." Or they will generate one religious "problem" after another, for which they seek counsel repeatedly. They shift their dependency to the counselor and make numerous telephone calls between interviews. If the counselor leaves the city for a business trip or a vacation, they are devastated—panicked—by their sense of abandonment. In fact, these persons may have three or four or more counselors at once without telling them about each other. Interviews and the telephone calls themselves are anxiety-allaying defenses against the fear of separation.

The Need for Magic Instead of Religion

The desperation of adults with a dependent personality disorder pushes them into periodic depressions. These times of depression are usually precipitated by a real loss or abandonment. Divorce or the death of a spouse are common examples.

A sixty-two-year-old widow had lost her husband about fourteen months previously, after his lingering illness with cancer. She had gone to live with her daughter because she could not stand to live alone. She had few friends of her own age and sex. She only occasionally went to church and then did not participate in any of the small-group study classes or semi-social groups. She was very isolated. She seemingly had gotten over the death of her husband, but her great worry was that she had committed the unpardonable sin. She asked her daughter to call the pastor and ask him to visit her. She was in bed when he arrived, although she was not under a doctor's care for any specific malady. She presented her worry about the unpardonable sin to the pastor.

The woman did very little Bible study and based her feeling about the unpardonable sin on sermons she had heard, usually by a television evangelist. Careful examination of the reassurances of scripture gave her little comfort and even failed to change the subject of her repetitious complaint about feeling terrified that she had committed a sin for which God would not forgive her. She kept expecting the pastor to say a "magic word" that would drive the thought away. The pastor read to her 1 John 3:19–20: "By this we shall know that we are of the truth, and reassure our hearts before him whenever our hearts condemn us; for God is greater than our hearts, and he knows everything." He prayed for relief from her unreasoning fear.

Before leaving, he conferred with the daughter. She was at her wits' end, not knowing how to help her mother. She said that in the last week five different pastors had come to the house. None had been any more successful in allaying her mother's distress. The daughter said that her father had "waited on Mother hand and foot" until the children got old enough to do so and then they were expected to take over. However, the mother was in good physical health! Now that her options for persons to wait on her were running out she had become depressed. She required psychiatric hospitalization for the depression, of which the demands for religious "magic words" were one expression. She had missed the whole point of the life of faith as a mutual bearing of burdens with fellow sufferers in responsible Christian fellowship. Her addictive dependency demanded instant solutions that left her with as little responsibility as possible. The death of her husband had thrown her dependent personality disorder off balance, a shift that resulted in a childishly naive belief in a religion of magical words. When her clinical depression lifted through combined psychiatric treatment and pastoral counseling, she was able to live productively in a retirement home, which she was able to afford. The organized group life of the home distributed the dependency over a responsible and larger number of people with an expert group therapist as a leader.

Forming Mutual Covenants with Dependent Persons

Tensions in relation to dependent persons surface in several different spheres of human relationships. Parents see the full-blown fruits of this way of life in sons or daughters who can't seem to get their act together in the years following graduation from high school or college. They make repeated forays into independent living but keep returning to the parental nest. College and professional school personnel meet dependent personalities in several ways. Some professors and administrators have these persons following them around constantly seeking advice, help, or even crisis intervention. A student may become enmeshed in his or her roommate's every move, and vice versa. These dependent personalities often shift their dependency from the parental home and become perpetual students, taking more and more courses, staying longer and longer in the embrace of their alma mater. A common result is for the college or university to give them a minor job on campus, and they squeeze by on a meager income indefinitely.

Husbands and wives in the early years of marriage may become aware for the first time how very dependent one is on the other, to the extent that it is a one-sided covenant—one partner is all give and the other is all take. The outside observer wonders whether this was a marriage or an adoption. The Cinderella syndrome in women and the Peter Pan syndrome in men are described in recent popular books about persons who live on the assumption that they are to be taken care of by their mate to the exclusion of the rest of the family's needs.

The dependent way of life has garden-variety expressions that prompt many people in the affluent culture of the last several decades to live their lives in quiet desperation. However, this way of life also has its more blatant expressions, probably the most common of which is addiction to drugs or alcohol. These addictions thrust the person into parasitism. Others, because of their sentimental devotion, may have fortunes wrung out of them "helping" the addict in a one-sided, defective covenant. Furthermore, chronic depression (with veiled threats of suicide) and feeble attempts at suicide are latently angry ways of reacting to expectations of family members and therapists that this person must begin to become more independent. Every move toward putting such persons on their own is read by them as abandonment.

What are some working strategies for building a responsible relationship of knowledgeable love with these persons? They are made in the image of God. They are persons for whom Christ died, and so are we. How can we care for them without contributing to their disordered existence and without being tyrannized by their living by proxy through us and other significant persons in their lives?

Considering Ourselves

In overtaking these persons in a way of life that is manifestly faulty, you and I must first consider ourselves. As a parent, you or I can ask, To what extent does this son or daughter's dependency feed my own insatiable need for him or her to be near me, to cater to my wishes, to do as I say, to give me a continued sense of being in control, a luxuriant sense of strength in the presence of my child's "need"? That "need" may be the external sign not of any real weakness on his or her part but of our own need to be needed. Why not meet that very natural need of mine by helping little babies who are in need? Why not address the real need of son or daughter to feel strength and competence as an adult? It is past time for cuddling them to ourselves.

The same self-examination is called for in professors, school administrators, counselors, and psychiatric team members. The teaching and the therapeutic relationship, separately or combined, are "bridge" relationships as the persons in our care move from one island of immaturity to a larger island of maturity until finally they come to the mainland of responsible adulthood. Responsible adulthood, in Jesus' teachings, means the capacity to accept the ministry of others as a gift, with abundant gratitude, but to be in the world primarily to minister and not to be ministered unto. We as care givers, be it dedicated friend, church school teacher, pastor, professor, psychotherapist, or a rare balancing of all these, first must come clean with ourselves before God as to our own need for the dependent person. When we get this straight, then we see ourselves as bridges over the person's troubled waters, but every *good* bridge has prominent "No Parking" signs on it!

Setting Limits That Stabilize Anxiety

A dependent son or daughter panics in the new responsibilities of college and returns home. Wise parents insist that he or she immediately begin looking for a job, after they have

carefully determined with reasonable amounts of tender loving care and medical attention that the son or daughter is not
ill. They may even provide counseling assistance on the condition that the young person take advantage of it. An outside
"coach," such as a wise counselor, may be of remarkable
assistance to the whole family system. But the parents do not
permit the son or daughter to sleep all day and hang out with
other idle friends all night. The apostle Paul wrote, "If any
one will not work, let him not eat" (2 Thess. 3:10). It may well
be that the son or daughter needs a psychological morato-
rium, as Erik Erikson aptly suggests, from school. He or she
may need to work at a variety of different jobs before going
to college. Now that the military draft of the Vietnam years is
not breathing down young people's necks, they can and
should be expected to do this if they opt out of college or high
school.

In many instances money is a factor in perpetuating dependency. College and professional school students, and especially graduate students on open-ended programs that have
no date for completion, tend to show their dependent personality disorders by draining their parents' budgets or expecting
a spouse, usually a wife, to finance their laid-back life-styles
as pseudo students. Alcohol and drug abusers usually have a
loved one or a succession of friends who bail them out of
drunken driving and automobile accident escapades. Undisciplined spendthrift behavior often is left undisciplined by the
"helpfulness" of some person with a ready checkbook who
cannot possibly let them go without. Grandparents are often
soft touches for wastrel married sons or daughters or grand-
children.

Parental overprotection tends to breed dependent ways of
life in growing persons. The implication of parental overprotection is that these persons are not capable of taking care of
themselves. They get the message, and their own initiative is
dulled or destroyed by a crippling sense of inferiority and
helplessness.

Teachers and therapists do not have unlimited time and
energy, and responsibilities for other students or patients
force them to set limits for the dependent person. Being on
twenty-four-hour availability contributes to the disorder
rather than changing it. A frank covenant about limits needs
to be established at the beginning of a relationship with a
dependent person, not later. A firm and clear, but kind, clarification of the goal of strengthening the person's self-confidence is the best of wisdom.

A Person-Centered Nondirectiveness

Carl Rogers, the eminent psychologist, developed a very influential process of counseling that he first called nondirective counseling and later reformulated as client-centered therapy. He applied it to areas such as personality growth and development, teaching, and human relations encounter groups. He hypothesized that the counselor or teacher does the most good for persons by (1) creating a nonthreatening relationship of genuine safety, (2) seeking to see the world from within the other person's world the way he or she sees it, (3) investing confidence in the person's own ability to make decisions and to carry them into action, and (4) avoiding replacing the person's own responsibility for his or her life by taking it over (Rogers 1951).

Such an approach, however, calls for a therapeutic or educational alliance on the part of the person seeking help. More recently Aaron Beck has produced remarkable results, especially with chronically depressed persons, in his research and practice of "cognitive therapy." One of the initial thrusts he suggests is that patients be encouraged and expected to believe that they themselves *can* be genuine partners in their own healing. They are not doomed to be dependent "things" to be "fixed" by someone else.

In pastoral counseling such expectations are translated into commitment to such persons' own relationship to God as one that enables them to work out their own salvation with fear and trembling. The plight of dependent persons before God is that they expect God to do everything for them without exerting faith in themselves and in God in order to rise up and be persons in their own right. God in Christ comes alongside us in the Holy Spirit, strengthening us with might in the inner person to will and to do what he has created us to be and to become. We go away sorrowing if we expect Christ to do everything for us while we atrophy and fail to express our faith in a living manner.

Calling Out and Affirming the Dependent Person's Gifts and Strengths

The major spiritual issue of dependent persons is denial of their own gifts and strengths. Such denial means that these gifts lie buried in their dependency upon others. When you or I become someone who "believes in them when they do not believe in themselves," the good news of God in Christ can become real to them. We become sons and daughters of encouragement, Barnabas-like persons. We collaborate with them instead of permitting them to feed our vanity with their vain sweetness and obsequious genuflections to our supposed all-powerfulness. We affirm their gifts and wait them out as they activate those gifts. We do not confront them in hostility but challenge them in gentle encouragement to believe that Jesus Christ endows those who believe in him with the power to become what they are potentially through the gifts God has bestowed on them.

Guidelines from Biblical Wisdom Literature for Relating to Dependent Persons

Some of what has been said already and much that has not yet been mentioned about relating effectively to dependent persons is brightly illuminated in the scriptures. Particularly is this true of the wisdom literature of the Old Testament and the parables of Jesus.

The technical literature repeatedly calls attention to the inner core of restless anxiety and lack of self-confidence in these persons. In the pressures and demands of day-to-day living, they borrow or counterfeit a self out of the images of the people upon whom they depend.

You and I are advised by Proverbs 20:5: "The purpose in a man's mind is like deep water, but a man of understanding will draw it out." We therefore look beyond the shallow waters of helplessness and low self-esteem to the deeper waters of anxiety and despair that they generate. We search the architectural and engineering design in these persons' "deep purpose," looking for their hidden strength. We may find it in the form of a neighbor, a teacher, or a pastor who understood and believed in them as adults other than and different from the saccharine-sweet Daddy's Little Girl or Mama's Little Lord Fauntleroy whom either the mother or father overprotects from their God-given right to stand on their own, to learn to make decisions and carry them out, and to become autonomous persons related directly to God as Providence. We persist on going to the depths of their well and finding the uniqueness, individuality, and creative strengths of the very image of God in them.

Then we can act on the wisdom of another proverb (Prov. 12:25): "Anxiety in a man's heart weighs him down, but a good word makes him glad." The *Good News Bible* translates the last line, "Kind words will cheer you up." The insight is further reinforced in *The Anchor Bible* translation of 15:13: "A happy heart lights up the face,/ But the spirit is lamed by an inner hurt."

Dependent persons have indeed been hurt by the lack of confidence in their own God-given strengths shown by those responsible for teaching them in the home, the church, and the school. You are that person of understanding who invests confidence in them with words of encouragement.

In the wisdom of Jesus' parable of the talents, we search for the servant whose master went on a journey and gave him one talent. When his master returned, he said, "I knew you to be a hard man, reaping where you did not sow, and gathering where you did not winnow; so I was afraid, and I went and hid your talent in the ground. Here you have what is yours" (Matt. 25:24–25). Let us get to such persons, if at all possible, when the decision is being made as to what to do with the real gift they have received. We respond to the terror that they feel and that impairs their judgment and freedom of action. Certainly we want to lay an encouraging hand on their shoulder while there is yet time. The capacity of spouses, employers, and all other "hard people" has not yet taken every vestige of courage from such persons and cast them aside in the competitive ratrace of our marketing culture. To these "hard people" only the bottom line counts. Nevertheless God loves and believes in those who have become dependent, because God made them. This harsh world is no friend to such grace or to the deep well of wisdom.

2

The Mask
of the Packaged Personality

The word "histrionic" is derived from the Latin word *histrio,* which means an actor. In recent psychiatric literature, histrionic has replaced the older term "hysterical" in describing personality. The word hysterical derives from the Greek *hystera,* meaning womb, giving the impression that the term is applicable only to women. Current writings on the subject, however, use the term histrionic to refer to both women and men. Either a woman or a man can follow an extremely other-directed, crowd-pleasing, star-performing, glittering, attention-getting way of life. Such persons are actors but seem never to be offstage, as contrasted with serious players who form lifelong and durable relationships of trust and loyalty with their loved ones, friends, and colleagues.

The histrionic man or woman is indeed akin to the person who follows a dependent way of life. However, histrionic persons are not *passively* dependent. They are aggressive scene stealers who manipulate others for their approval and attention and who express forcefully their need of others' praise. They do not, as Millon says, place "their fate in the hands of others, . . . thereby having their security in constant jeopardy" (Millon 1981:131). Through many seductive ways they maneuver, manipulate, exert pressure, and maintain many "masks" to exact what they need and want from others.

Yet they are nicely packaged people. They are seriously impaired in the capacity to form and maintain steadfast, loyal, and durable relationships with the same person or persons over a long period of time, certainly not over a lifetime. They are summer patriots in superficial, short-lived liaisons.

The Social and Religious "Market"
for Packaged Personalities

Erich Fromm assesses our culture as an American people. He considers the histrionic personality of our times as a "marketing character":

> For the marketing character everything is transformed into a commodity—not only things, but the person himself, his physical energy, his skills, his knowledge, his opinions, his feelings, even his smiles. (Fromm 1973:349)

In another work (1947:69–78), Fromm is more specific:

> Success depends largely upon how well a person sells himself on the market, how well he gets his personality across, how nice a package he is; whether he is cheerful, sound, aggressive, reliable, ambitious. . . . The premise of the marketing orientation is emptiness, the lack of any specific quality which should not be subject to change.

Within the religious community we have the end result of this endemic way of life of a nation. In the churches we are aided and abetted in religious histrionics through our emulation of television's political and social demand for "cosmetic leadership," flashy first impressions of people who have a "marketable image." With preachers and pastors as well as lawyers, politicians, and salespersons we are left to wonder who that person *is* behind that mask! We pray for release from cynicism. Yet we wonder if this person will not also simply have been putting on an act for our temporary approval in order to get where he or she wants to go, or to get what he or she wants to get out of us. All the while, within the person there is an emptiness, a craving for new conquests, new stimulation, additional applauding audiences. In a poignant way they are, as T. S. Eliot describes them, "hollow" persons. Boredom is their constant, sad motivator. Only occasionally are they aware that this is their plight.

The Patterning of the Histrionic Way of Life

Histrionic persons are lively and dramatic, exaggerate a great deal, and thereby overdramatize whatever they are describing. They overreact, their behavior being out of all proportion to the particular stimulating event, person, or thing. They constantly crave new stimulation and excitement and easily become bored with the routines of life and work.

In relation to people they are apt to be perceived as shallow and lacking in genuineness, even if superficially charming and appealing. They may "quickly form friendships [but] once a relationship is established, they often become either demanding, egocentric, and inconsiderate, which may result in manipulative suicidal threats, gestures, or attempt" (Millon 1981:132).

When we pay attention to the way they relate to the opposite sex both within and outside of marriage, we quickly see that histrionic persons are frequently strikingly charming, tend to dress with a startling showiness, and seductively seek to control the opposite sex. They do this by entering into a relationship with a sexual partner under a facade of dependency. The woman's helplessness with a "big strong man" and the man's line that builds her up, or both of their flights into romantic fantasy, make the relationship illusory and transient. DSM III (p. 314) refuses to identify these behaviors with women alone: "In both sexes overt behavior is a caricature of femininity. The actual quality of their sexual relationships is variable. Some individuals are promiscuous, others naive and sexually unresponsive, and others have an apparently normal sexual life." Millon adds (1981:140), "In the sphere of sexuality . . . many histrionics are quite at ease when 'playing the game' but become confused, immature, and apprehensive when matters get serious."

One recurrent complaint of histrionic persons is that they have vague and difficult-to-diagnose physical ailments. For example, when caught in an embarrassing or humiliating situation, they may break out in hives or develop nausea, or previously existing disorders will either flare up anew or intensify if already present. Earlier medical opinion tended to make this their primary problem, but more recently, with more sophisticated studies of stress, such persons' somatic or physical complaints are regarded as less significant than the unsatisfactory features of their inner and interpersonal way of life.

Religious Manifestations of the Histrionic Way of Life

The Histrionic Church Pastor or Staff Person

In the context of the parish, the histrionic way of life finds many religious expressions and almost as many social reinforcements.

I have been a consultant to church boards and to both pastors and individual lay members of churches. In these settings I have observed that personnel decisions of search committees and denominational pastor-church relations counselors are highly complicated by candidates who make marvelous first impressions and sweep the committee and congregation off their feet. They present themselves in over-dramatized ways, make dashing first impressions, and vigilantly respond to the most subtle cues of the individuals and groups with whom they talk in such a way as to please them initially.

The irony of the situation is that the congregations themselves want a gregarious, outgoing, charming pastor, minister of music, or minister of education, and especially someone to "work with the youth." More careful expectation of a person who forms relationships responsibly, makes promises carefully on the basis of plenty of information, and is able to stick with people through longer, less superficial relationships is not a high priority for many churches when they select leaders. As a result, careless and poorly inspected covenants are formed with leader after leader. The church can recite a litany of complaints about their last one, two, three, or four pastors, who came for a short while and left. They got bored and became boring!

However, behavior of much more significance led up to the church pastor or staff member leaving. Immediately upon assuming the assigned duties, the new person began making dramatic changes in the way things had always been done. When resistance arose, he or she responded with emotional upset. This turned into angry outbursts or tantrums. The complaint may be that church people are suspicious of anything new. They want to do things the old way. They are set in their ways. The new pastor craves novelty, stimulation, and excitement. It is a catch-22!

A church and a prospective pastor can avoid this if they take great care in forming their covenants about what changes the new person will make and on what kind of timetable. In congregational forms of church government this is very difficult to do. Open covenants need to be communicated thoroughly to the whole church. When all the members of a search committee are caught up by the contagious histrionics of the prospective pastor or staff member, they fail to make a clear, careful covenant of expectation with the candidate. Then, too, they are busy people with full-time jobs, not to mention a certain naïveté in perceiving what they want to perceive in the candidate without checking things out.

Sexual Acting-Out in Churches

Religious services are not immune to erotic excitation. Some parish church services and some televised "religious shows" are replete with seductive clothing, music, bodily movement, and overdramatized religiosity in the order of the service. In contrast to such histrionic overlays, the life of Jesus is starkly tragic and dramatic. These exaggerated displays set the atmosphere for individual acting-out of superficial and shallow sexual behavior in private.

Histrionic life-styles are prevalent in these behaviors within the fellowship of the church. Liaisons occur between members who are close to the ministerial leadership and laypersons who are active in the leadership of the church. Sometimes they happen between members of official boards. Proximity and ease of access both in church buildings and each other's homes can easily turn a sentimental religious attachment into an erotic involvement. In studying such cases, you will often find that one or the other or both persons involved has a history of superficial, short-term liaisons of whatever kind before the present instance.

Sometimes a pastor will become involved sexually with a histrionic person in pastoral visitation or counseling. The real antidote for this is carefully to assess and control the initiative, the time, and the place when and where the person is visited or a counseling hour is given. Here again it is imperative to inspect carefully each highly dramatic demand of a church member or anyone else who asks for a pastor's time and attention. This inspection clarifies the degree of emergency that in reality the person is facing. (To the histrionic person *everything* is an emergency!) The inspection also includes closely inquiring about the place where you will meet the person, as well as the discreetness and appropriateness of the meeting time. Without this, confusion, panic, and immaturity will saturate this very awkward situation, with many people catching the contagion of the histrionic person and being manipulated by it. A pastor either can get caught up in the panicky exaggeration of a minor event into a major catastrophe, or the pastor can slow it down, inspect it, and not let such persons take control.

These last sentences apply equally for the layperson in a church whose pastor or minister of music, education, or youth keeps things stirred up by the teacup tempests of exaggerated and overdramatized crises he or she presents to you. You can use the same coolheaded, evenhanded inspection. The transactional-analysis work of Eric Berne carefully describes the maneuvers of the histrionic person as repeatedly playing the game of Uproar. He says these games are part of a larger "script": a life pattern based on decisions made in childhood, reinforced and rewarded or justified by subsequent events, and issuing in deceptive games as a habitual way of life (Berne 1972:446).

Religious expressions of love, intimacy, caring, fellowship, and personal sharing and testimony can easily become eroticized and promiscuous. First Timothy 5:1–2 gives some timely wisdom to the churches and their leaders: "Do not rebuke an older man but exhort him as you would a father; treat younger men like brothers, older women like mothers, younger women like sisters." Contemporary psychotherapeutic wisdom alludes to and amplifies this advice. Churches can become incestuous, abusive, intermeshings of families bringing all their scripts with them. If these spiritual kinspersons in the church are to be treated as one would treat blood relatives, then wisdom and discernment are imperative. The more we know about the multigenerational family of these persons, the more we can anticipate their response and the less likely we will be to reinforce the immaturities they brought with them. The more we understand just how we were treated by and treated our fathers, mothers, brothers, and sisters, the more wisely we can relate to fellow church members.

Some clinical observations of physicians and pastoral counselors who have observed histrionic girls point to a causal relationship between physical symptoms of episodes of amnesia, brain-lesionless seizures, and psychological symptoms of depression, suicide attempts, and running away from home. The girl and her mother would have a dark secret and neither would report the fact that the father, stepfather, or live-in boyfriend was regularly abusing the daughter sexually.

In our clinic we discover that behind many cases of histrionic behavior patterns in young adulthood lies a long history of incestuous sexual abuse. This can be found in both men and women, although women are more often afflicted. That the church leadership not add to this history with more secret sexual exploitation is an imperative of the gospel and of all ministers free of the crime of pastoral malpractice.

I have noticed that these histrionic persons still carry this sexual abuse as a secret. As a result they have a habitual territoriality staked out around their person. They form superficial relationships out of fear of the ultimate predator.

They keep their body space free from invasion and become rigid and somewhat panicked when someone touches them.

Some Other Influential Experiences of Histrionic Men and Women

Sealed-Off Memory

Underneath their apparent shallowness and avoidance of an inner life, histrionic persons have an impaired memory of their encounters with others. When you are out of their sight, you are out of their mind. They have moved on to a newer stimulus or experience. This is why they may be lacking in faithfulness to promises and loyalty to persons with whom they have made a covenant and to whom they have made promises.

Biogenic Factors

No convincing case has been made for any constitutional or biochemical factor in these people's neurological makeup. From birth they are reported to be "high-strung" and "emotionally sensitive." While we await further medical studies, we have little substantial data to back a parent or other relative's "heredity" rationalization of the adult histrionic's erratic behavior.

Family History

Following John Bowlby's monumental studies of attachment, separation, and loss, combined with clinical histories of people with histrionic life-styles, we can hypothesize from reliably gathered information that they have been bounced from pillar to post in growing up. They may have been in a family that often moved from place to place. They formed quick but shallow friendships; they knew they would be there only a short time, so why invest? Or these persons may have lived in the same geographical territory as their friends but were handed back and forth among many care givers in life—parents, older siblings, uncles and aunts, grandparents, and even friendly neighbors who took a liking to them. Foster home placements also participate in short-term, superficial relationships. In such transient situations, the growing person is always a sort of guest, an outsider. He or she may find that use of charm, covert hinting, and outright manipulation are the only ways to make it in someone else's territory. Very early the habit of sealing off one's own feelings and internal communications is a necessary coping style. Just doing what you know or think will please these people as a good guest in their house is the way to survive.

Parental "Show and Tell" Needs

David Elkind has made much of today's "hurried child." There are parents who for their own gratification will put their child on display in front of audiences long before the child is emotionally ready for it. Their paternal approval of the child depends on his or her ability and willingness to be an actor of one kind or another. They may spend excessive amounts of time with the child, dressing, grooming, and making the child "look pretty." Histrionics-in-the-making are pushed into public speaking, singing, or performing. Churches interpret success at this as a sign of God calling them to the ministry. Less dramatic signs often go unnoticed. Parents also see it as parental success that maybe God is calling the person to be a minister or a "Christian entertainer."

In the larger community, ballet performances, music recitals, football games, and beauty contests are stages onto which the child is pushed. As Millon says, "The parents of future histrionic persons rarely punish their children, they distribute rewards only for what they approve and admire, but they often fail to bestow these rewards even when the child behaves well" (Millon 1981:152).

I have watched these phenomena in many generations of seminary students and medical students who are sons or daughters of prominent people. Their parents themselves are in the spotlight as a result of their way of making a living. Ministers, lawyers, actors, and politicians are all "beholden to their constituency" to make a good impression, to look good, to keep up appearances, no matter what. The show must go on! By association, children imitate and take this behavior as their own—with their personal caricatures of it as well. Some of these caricatures become a source of high humor. Others become humiliating.

For example, a mother and father in very active lay leadership positions in their church are greatly pleased when their daughter decides to enter full-time religious work. She hopes to be a foreign missionary, a cause her parents ardently support. Everything goes well until the daughter becomes actively involved in a civil rights struggle for blacks in their community. The parents do not punish her. They simply withhold approval of her working with "niggers." To add to the situation, the daughter enters seminary, falls in love with an Oriental man, and marries him. This alarms the parents. She is not imitating them in a way that makes them happy. She is obedient to their teachings, but they feel humiliated!

The Spiritual Plight of the Histrionic Man or Woman

The plight of histrionic persons at the verbal level is one of global overdramatization of superficial concerns. They do this by universalizing their spiritual outlook. If someone has betrayed them, then *all* people are liars, they say in their haste, as did the psalmist in Psalm 116:11. The one person whom they perceive to have lied to them does not make all persons liars. This generalization is an unthought-out statement. If the person has been jilted by a lover, he or she is likely to say, "My life is over! All men [or women] out there are jerks."

The general semanticists are very helpful to a pastoral counselor or a layperson in the church. They suggest that we firmly but gently challenge the global "all or nothing" responses of people—responses like "all," "everybody," "nothing," "never," "always," "nobody," and the like. We can do so with queries such as: "Is there not at least one person you know who is different from what you have just said?" The object is to push them back into themselves for some reflective thought. The New Testament gift we are trying to stimulate in them is the gift of discernment, which enables them to distinguish between good and evil in a reflective way. (See 1 Cor. 12:10; Heb. 5:11–14; and 1 John 4:1.) In their marriage, discernment can be translated as considerateness or dwelling together according to knowledge and not with global broadsides at each other ("She never does anything right!"). (See 1 Peter 3:7.)

Another spiritual concern is the inner emptiness of the histrionic patient. This is the end result of a life without commitment. A marriage enrichment group can go a long way toward creating an atmosphere of trust in which these people—with a clearly understood contract that they are committed to see the group process through to the end—can begin to fill up some of the emptiness by relating to each other as persons in Christ and not as commodities to be pushed around. C. G. Jung's often-quoted statement that his patients over the age of forty regularly were suffering from the lack of a meaningful faith suggests something of the crisis of an existential vacuum in people's lives. I have noticed that innumerable persons come for counseling between the ages of thirty-eight and forty-two complaining of boredom with their job and with their marital partner. They are considering divorce and possibly a job change at the same time.

If you define the counseling situation as a search for a new spiritual grasp on life, you encourage persons to deepen their commitment to God and then, using that as a guideline, to decide who they really are and what under God is their destiny. This will help them reshape their whole interpretation of life. The objective is to challenge the spiritual emptiness and poverty of thought with which they are facing two great issues: work and love. The steadfastness of our own relationship as counselors to them is the catalyst. Family therapy can often enhance this process by involving other members as a working system in the decisions, commitments, and dedications that are made.

The whole theological concern of consecration and the development of what Josiah Royce called "the philosophy of loyalty" is the primary healing grace for the histrionic's struggle on "life's wild, restless sea."

Biblical Wisdom and Perspective for Caring for Histrionic Men and Women

One recurrent ethical issue appears in our discussion of the histrionic's plight. The issue focuses on the person's dealing with other people. Furthermore, when it appears in the religious community, in its expectations of its membership and leadership, a serious spiritual gap has been left in the teaching of the gospel of the redemption offered us in the life, death, burial, and resurrection of Jesus Christ.

That recurrent ethical and spiritual issue is the deathless durability of our spiritual covenant with God and each other in Christ. This stands in stark contrast with the brevity, fickleness, lack of durability, lack of fidelity and loyalty, and short memory of promises made that we find in our study of the histrionic way of life. If an individual is found to be a histrionic person, then, to paraphrase Isaiah, he or she is a person of a histrionic way of life and lives in a church and community of a histrionic way of life. In this church and community he or she peddles the wares of a "market orientation" in a clamoring marketplace. Once again, the more we consider the aberrant behavior of individuals, the further away from the doctor and other therapists we get and the nearer we get to the schools and their teachers, the churches and their ministers, and the homes with their parents in residence. How can we deal with both the individual and the community as we pray for healing of our histrionic way of life? How can we deal gently with the ignorant and wayward and confess our own participation in this way of life ourselves? Let me suggest several things from the biblical wisdom we have at our fingertips all the time.

Steadfastness as a Christian Virtue

We challenge the lack of durability in the histrionic way of life with the stick-to-itiveness and long-term commitment called *steadfastness* in the scriptures. Hebrews 6:17–20 states this with unmistakable clarity:

> So when God desired to show more convincingly to the heirs of the promise the unchangeable character of his purpose, he interposed with an oath, so that through two unchangeable things, in which it is impossible that God should prove false, we who have fled for refuge might have strong encouragement to seize the hope set before us. We have this as a sure and steadfast anchor of the soul, a hope that enters into the inner shrine behind the curtain, where Jesus has gone as a forerunner on our behalf, having become a high priest for ever after the order of Melchizedek.

The intrinsic nature of the Christian faith is to provide an anchoring hope of a sure and steadfast relationship to God in Jesus Christ and to each other. The ethical imperative of the work of Christ as our "forerunner" is steadfastness and loyalty. Paul concludes his extensive theological discussion of the resurrection with the ethical instruction: "Therefore, my beloved brethren, be steadfast, immovable, always abounding in the work of the Lord, knowing that in the Lord your labor is not in vain" (1 Cor. 15:58).

This character trait of steadfastness Erik Erikson calls fidelity. In the development of human personality, the strength of fidelity is at its peak testing time in adolescence. The particular ego strength of fidelity is formed in the crucible of the young person's "double uncertainty of a newly matured sexual machinery which must be kept in abeyance in some or all of its functions while he prepares for his own place in the adult order." The person is put to the test of developing an inner coherence and a durable set of values. Then Erikson defines fidelity as "the ability to sustain loyalties freely pledged in spite of the inevitable contradictions of value systems" (Erikson 1964:124–125).

In the contemporary religious community, we need an agonizing reappraisal of the "formal" teachings of adolescents. In the home, the church, and the school they have a hidden curriculum of recreation, especially superficial and recreational sex, showmanship as a mark of religiosity, and hurrying into adulthood. We have only sporadic demands that they be loyal to each other's best interests at the cost of personal denial of the fickle wishes that pressure them at the moment. "Abounding in the work of the Lord" places steadfastness above temporary thrills. Fidelity in the responsible use of their bodies, automobiles, and mind-altering substances, and in the promises they make, calls for the balanced attention of parents and church leaders to their rapidly forming decision-making habits. This involves a dramatic shift from legalistic rules to negotiated covenants with an adolescent: mutual covenants between a parent or parents and an emerging adult son or daughter, faithfully monitored, reviewed, and kept. Revision of these covenants is the first line of defense against the histrionic way of life. Frankly making this the formal curriculum and doing away with the hidden curriculum in church meetings and activities also will go a long way toward challenging the histrionic way of life. The inner life of the emerging young adult need not remain a hollow shell of appearances without an inner core of integrity and personal loyalty to an adult way of life among his or her peers.

This inner core of integrity has an outward expression in both adolescents and adults in the durability and stability of the friendships they form. The church's belief formally stated is that in the resurrection community, faith, hope, and love remain. These endure. They are built on covenants carefully formed and diligently maintained, renegotiated at new levels of growth. These durable relationships, in turn, enrich the lives of the people of God as the vicissitudes of illness, disappointments, wars, personal abandonment, advancing old age and infirmity, and death strike them. These covenantal relationships transcend the geographical boundaries of life, the rapid movement of people from one place to another, and their shifting occupational and family locations.

When the importance of personal loyalty is introduced to histrionic persons of any age, they are at least challenged to open up the gates of a new life of depth rather than superficiality, durability rather than transiency. It begins with our own personal relationship to them: Will we be just another person who is seduced by their flashy blandishments, only to be abandoned later? Will we be just another person who will let their restless boredom go unchallenged and unconfronted? Will we be just another person who lets them use us while we use them for our own purposes in return? Will a durable and steadfast relationship of fidelity be our goal, both stated and acted upon? Or will we let them get away with threatening to have done with our company rather than change their ways, as John Bunyan puts it so well? One of the most important tests of character and maturity is the capacity of a person to form and maintain *lasting* relationships.

3

The Mask
of Self-Assurance

People with dependent and histrionic life-styles draw their strength and direction from other people to the exclusion of developing an inner personal autonomy and self-direction. Self-absorbed persons wish little or nothing from others, except that which gratifies their appetite for adulation and confirmation of their superiority. They live a self-admiring and self-sufficient way of life. They despise weakness and dependency. They draw their sense of security and satisfaction from being above the crowd, disdainful of and superior to other people—stronger, brighter, more beautiful, wealthier, less fallible, and certainly more important than others. This self-estimate is a naive, unexamined, but tenaciously held assumption of the self-absorbed, narcissistic life-style.

In Christian theology, this is—more consistently than sexual concupiscence—the stuff of which original sin is made. Hubris, or self-elevation, is, as Milton put it, humankind's first disobedience to God. In catalogs of deadly sins, pride is the parent sin. We shall be as God, totally self-contained, self-sufficient, and needing no one and nothing from anyone. (The picture of God in this fantasy is that of a complete "aseity," i.e., total self-containment. This is a far cry from the Jewish concept of the Suffering Servant or the Christian belief in the sacrificial character of the Christ. God in Christ participates fully in our suffering. At the same time, God's grace in Christ is sufficient to release us from the bondage of our self-absorption.) The cryptic thread of narcissism runs through all our natures. In the self-absorbed or narcissistic way of life, though, it is not just a thread; it is the controlling pattern and motif of one's assumptions about oneself in relation to God and other people. As Millon says, "Narcissists need depend on no one else for gratification;

there is always themselves to 'keep themselves warm' " (Millon 1981:169).

Some Hallmarks of the Self-Absorbed Way of Life

The term "narcissism," used by psychologists and psychiatrists, has a history in Greek mythology. Narcissus was an extremely handsome young man. A young girl named Echo fell desperately in love with him, but he held himself aloof from her in nonchalant and cool indifference. Before long she wasted away and died because of his indifference.

That is not the end of the story. Nemesis, the goddess of retributive justice—the one who pays you back full measure and more for the evil you have done—punished Narcissus' indifference to Echo by causing him to fall in love with his own image as he saw it reflected in the pool of a fountain. She caused Narcissus to pine away in desire for his own reflection. He was then changed into the flower that bears his name.

This self-absorption is normal in a helpless infant, whose first acquaintance with "need" is for air, warmth, and food. As one physician described his own newborn son, "He is a ravenous appetite at one end and a total sense of irresponsibility at the other end!" Even in the "magic years" of early childhood, a youngster lives as Alice in Wonderland did, "in a world of her own." A childish sense of all-powerfulness and limitlessness rules the imagination. The seamy and rough edges of living in the world with parents, brothers and sisters, and playmates shake and frustrate these illusions.

When a person carries these self-absorbed assumptions past childhood, through school years, and into adult life, the behavior they generate is no longer "cute," "darling," and "sweet." It may remain so to doting parents who continue to reinforce it, but not to the rest of the world. What are some forms this behavior takes? A brief interpretation of the criteria of diagnosis of a narcissistic personality disorder reveals a descriptive profile.

Inflated Self-Esteem

Self-absorbed persons are masters of exaggeration of their own accomplishments. They arrogantly overstate their talents. They pretentiously show off a blatant self-assurance. They are brassy, full of chutzpah, and nothing to the contrary of their self-estimate is heard, much less acknowledged. If indeed they *are* persons of remarkable good looks or high intelligence and have mastered a skill, an art, or a profession, then they tend to make their case for themselves stick; it seems plausible. Yet *the capacity for self-evaluation and self-criticism is absent* in any case. Consequently, the self-absorbed leader in churches, in politics, in medicine, and in international affairs is likely to project his or her narcissism onto a large screen of public adulation.

Lack of Empathy for and Exploitation of Other People

Self-absorbed persons use other people to indulge their desires. They live lives of grandly assumed "entitlement," believing that what others do for them is only what they deserve and what they are entitled to. To expect such persons to show genuine gratitude or to do favors in return is like expecting a person with no arms to shake hands with you. Reciprocal covenants, genuine social contracts of mutual service, are not made by such people. The personal integrity and rights of others are disregarded while at the same time special favors are expected, assumed, or demanded.

The "exploitative orientation" is Erich Fromm's graphic name for the self-absorbed person. Such a person "does not expect to receive things from others as a gift, but to take them away by force or cunning" (Fromm 1947:64). Self-absorbed persons tend to enjoy only those features of "connections" with people that they have taken from others. The poignant spiritual deficit is a lack of awareness of grace and an incapacity for gratitude.

The capacity for empathy, for putting oneself in another person's place and experiencing that person's needs as primary, is missing in the narcissistic personality. In the religious sphere of behavior, God is no exception to the exploitation by the self-absorbed person. As Browning described such persons, they perceive God "as a purveyor to their appetites." And as Augustine described it, "Good men use the world to enjoy God, whereas bad men use God to enjoy the world" (*De Doctrina Christiana* 22.20). These persons seek to control God. It does not occur to them to yield control of their world to God. Religion is magic, and the narcissist is the magician.

A Grandiose Imagination

Self-absorbed persons are full of big ideas couched in glowing terms but with little detail as to exactly how these ideas will be put into specific, concrete action. They are more likely to be preoccupied with the big idea's unlimited possibilities. Søren Kierkegaard describes these persons as being "intoxicated with possibility." It can be added that the underside of this intoxication is their extreme vulnerability when faced with "putting up or shutting up" on some of these extravagant notions. In such instances they will fake it, make elaborate promises, not fulfill them, and fall into a severe misunderstanding with the "stupid" and "inferior" people who got in the way of their fulfillment of a long-cherished dream. Kierkegaard's understanding is again precise when he notes the despair that such an "infinite dreamer" falls into when overtaken by the hard necessities of life. Only scapegoats can protect this fragile paper house of egotism.

Arrogant Unflappableness

Unless the enormous self-confidence of self-absorbed persons is drastically thrown off balance, they appear consistently to be coolly unimpressed by the "pedestrian" achievements of those about them. This nonchalance and aloof detachment seems only to goad lovers of the opposite sex to try a little harder to impress and push another into a passionate commitment. All the while the self-absorbed person is coldly figuring out what this man or woman "can do for me." Indeed, there may be several simultaneous such liaisons. Not by chance, then, is the name "Don Juan" applied to men of this self-absorbed life-style. Whereas similar cool nonchalance appears in self-absorbed women, no specific code name seems to have stuck, with the possible exception of "La Belle Dame Sans Merci" ("The Beautiful Lady Without Mercy") of Alain Chartier and John Keats. This arrogant unflappableness is a mask of sanity masquerading as serenity. Behind it lies a deeply impaired capacity for commitment to other persons.

A Deficient Social Conscience

The ordinary rules of human interaction are set aside by self-absorbed persons. They are exceptions, and people who insist upon treating them like anybody else just do not understand or appreciate who they are. DSM III says that they "flout conventions of shared living and disregard the personal integrity and rights of others." The apostle Paul contended with this mood of being exempt from the ethical demands of the gospel in his letters to the Corinthians and Romans. Some of those people said to themselves and each other, "All things are lawful for me" (1 Cor. 6:12). Others, taking the liberation from Jewish law as a license to do as they pleased, said, "Let us sin all the more that grace may abound" (cf. Rom. 6:1–2). This was called "antinomianism," or living without norms, code, or ethical obligations. The self-absorbed narcissist lives *above* the law. It is beneath his or her station in life. It might be better to call such persons "supranomians."

If anyone realistically accepts the strictures of time, the accommodations that it takes to live in a give-and-take reciprocity with other people and abide by rules of considerateness of other people's well-being—that person will be in severe conflict with the narcissist. The alternatives for existing peacefully and without confrontation are few: to ignore self-absorbed persons, to stay out of any contractual negotiations with them, or to listen without responding as they boast and compliment themselves. Some people have a rare sense of humor and can get away with humorous responses that border on sarcasm. Ordinarily, the self-absorbed are so deadly serious in their expansive fantasies that humor is met with hostility or rage. To burst their balloon prompts a surly irritability, with spells of being down in the mouth, embarrassed, and empty.

Religious Expressions of the Self-Absorbed Way of Life

The religious garb or "cosmetics" of the narcissistic way of life is usually glossy but thick overlays of a religiosity that protests too much.

"God Is at My Beck and Call"

The prayer claim that God will do exactly as they ask with no regard to the kind of claims God has on them is a common type of religious behavior of narcissistic persons. Elaborate explanations of what God has "done for me" cause struggling realists to furrow their brows, wag their heads, and sigh. "Why is this person so special to God?" they wonder. This becomes exploitative when such persons begin to issue demands to a spouse, a fellow church member, or a television or radio audience, arising out of "private talks" they have had with God. This corruption of prayers of petition and intercession manipulates and coerces other people, many of whom fall prey to the tender trap of narcissistic religiosity. The narcissist believes so definitely that "God is at my beck and call" that many people are taken in by such colossal self-assurance.

In marketplace theology, it is as Wordsworth said: "The world is too much with us; late and soon,/ Getting and spending, we lay waste our powers." Prayer easily is perceived as "getting," a question of what God can "do for me." The other dimensions of prayer as adoration, communion, self-examination, clarification, and a mutual co-laboring with God are neglected. The validity of prayer is put to the test in terms of our being able to turn stones into bread, being all-powerful, and being able to jump off high places without being hurt (Luke 4:1–14). Exemption, being entitled to preferential treatment by God in the face of illness, becomes the sole basis of the validity of prayer and acceptance of the reality of God. In the narcissistic prayer, bad things may happen to good people, but such things simply do not happen to perfect people like themselves. They are entitled to preferential treatment.

The Authoritarian Personality's Claim of Infallibility

A much more serious and less easily detected religious behavior of narcissism is the authoritarian religious person's claim to the infallibility of his or her particular religious beliefs. The vast qualitative difference between clarity and depth of religious convictions, on the one hand, and the arrogant claim to infallibility on the other is seen in the character traits of openness, empathy, teachability, and humility toward the beliefs of other people. These traits are foreign to narcissistic persons. Instead, they clothe their beliefs in vociferous claims of the infallibility of a particular church, book, theory, ritual, etc.

This behavior is not limited to religious people, and neither are religious people any less immune to it than are others. For example, economists can become high priests of a particular economic theory that they hold to be infallible. Medical doctors can attribute infallibility to a particular treatment modality for a given disorder. Business entrepreneurs can lay claim to the infallibility of their corporation, pointing to its manifest destiny. Authoritarian heads of state can proclaim the infallibility of their particular form of government.

Neither politically nor religiously does the narcissism of the authoritarian person restrict itself to the smoke screens of such catchwords as "liberal," "conservative," or "fundamentalist." Self-absorbed egotism can shift from one to another of these rhetorics at will. There seems to be, in the swinging pendulum of religious and political life, a lurching self-correction course. The thesis of one narcissistic authoritarianism lurches against the antithesis of another kind of authoritarianism. Yet the component of self-absorbed narcissism infects the new thesis that arises. Extremism demands the rejection of self-criticism, teachability in relation to those who have another angle of vision, and empathy toward the weaker one in the power game of self-aggrandizement. As Eric Hoffer says (1951:51):

> The inordinately selfish . . . separate the excellent instrument of their selfishness from their ineffectual selves and attach it to the service of some holy cause. And though it be a faith of love and humility they adopt, they can neither be loving nor humble.

A subtle transformation takes place in religious behavior when this happens. The unrealistic idealization of Jesus, for example, is pushed to such finespun logic that Jesus is viewed and portrayed as being completely different from struggling humans like us, who have to learn what we know and earn what we eat. To them he was so completely informed and sustained by the automatic control of God, as indeed were those who reported the events of his life, that he and they were exempt from the ordinary stresses of learning and earning that we must face. This is a modern version of ancient Gnosticism, teaching in effect that the Christ only *seemed* to be human, to have lived the life of sacrifice and died the death of the cross.

The strange and curious way that self-absorbed religionists make use of Gnostic conviction enables them to preach, teach, and espouse the shimmering ideal of belief in the Christ and the infallibility of those who recorded his story. At the same time, they consider themselves personally exempt from the ordinary rules of conduct that portray the way Jesus lived and the teachings we must abide by if we would live effectively with God and our neighbor.

This massive exemption relieves self-absorbed authoritarian personalities of any need for consistency. They can do as they please in pursuing their goals of self-gratification in the name of Christ. They can exploit other people's financial means, sexual being, social position, or anything else as long as it fulfills their infallible claims. The infallibility is now *theirs!*

The wisdom of Gandhi, who held that one of our strongest allies is that part of our enemy which is *right,* pinpoints the fatal flaw in the religious authoritarian personality. Without the wisdom that comes from critics, we are denied the fruits of both listening to and being heard by people who are different from us. As Tennyson put it, we "shut ourselves within ourselves and let the devil pipe his own." We spend our lives listening only to what we want to hear.

Consequently, the narcissistic religious person who attracts a following of other people will almost always shut off communication of that group with outsiders. The stranger, the person who is not "one of us," is not perceived as a person to be carefully entertained as an emissary or angel whom God has sent to us. A secret guardian or group of guardians must spy the stranger out and get incriminating data on how the stranger is different. Indeed, even members of the in-group must be tested repeatedly for their loyalty.

In this kind of narcissistic religious atmosphere, outsiders or disloyal persons become increasingly expendable. The seeds of violence in a family, a church, a denomination, a political group, or a nation germinate. Any act of reprisal becomes not only right but sanctioned by God.

Probably the most gruesome case of the narcissistic religious way of life in recent history was the Peoples Temple of San Francisco led by Jim Jones. The culmination of this reflection of the culture of narcissism in the mass suicide and murder of over 900 people shocked the world. The waves of violence and terrorism that reverberate over the world now tend to have a deep religious motivation. People kill to do God a favor, and suicide becomes a way of salvation.

Biblical Wisdom and the Self-Absorbed Way of Life

One of the missing spiritual vitamins for the well-being of individuals and groups within the Christian community is the strong wisdom wrought out of daily living that characterizes both the Old and the New Testament witness to the presence of God as infinite intelligence and wisdom. The human mind is the "candle of the Lord." The wisdom literature of the Bible, such as Proverbs and Ecclesiastes in the Old Testament and the sayings and parables of Jesus and Paul and the pastoral epistles in the New Testament, tends to accentuate the difference between the fool and the wise person. The disuse and abuse of the gifts of intelligence with which God has made us is a concern of these wisdom treatises, and it illuminates our understanding of these personality disorders. It creates a dialogue between religion and the psychiatric data pertaining to the character and the way of life of people as seen in every illness to which they fall prey.

The problems of the narcissistic or self-absorbed way of life are carefully identified by the apostle Paul. He admits his own fallibility, saying that he knows "in part" (1 Cor. 13:12). He distinguishes between his own opinion and the "command of the Lord" (1 Cor. 7:25). He readily asserts his credentials as a Jew, saying that he has reason for his self-confidence, but he counts it as loss, admitting he has suffered the loss of all this and counted these things as refuse in order to gain Christ (Phil. 3:4ff.). In speaking of his "thorn in the flesh," Paul describes its presence in his life as a curb against his self-elevation or "boasting," by which, as he says, "there is nothing to be gained." He has refrained from it "so that no one may think more of me than he sees in me or hears from me." The thorn in the flesh has kept him from being too elated or arrogant (2 Cor. 12:1–10).

In his wisdom about one's self-estimate, Paul says, "If any one thinks he is something, when he is nothing, he deceives himself. But let each one test his own work, and then his reason to boast will be in himself alone and not in his neighbor" (Gal. 6:3–4). Paul is most precise in his assessment of self-absorption when he says, "But when they measure themselves by one another, and compare themselves with one another, they are without understanding" (2 Cor. 10:12).

When we turn to Jesus' temptations in the wilderness, we see the massive discipline of his own person in the pressure of the tempter's appeal to his human self-centering possibility. In his profound perception of the self-centered possibilities of prayer, he tells the parable of the Pharisee and the publican praying: "The Pharisee stood and prayed thus *with himself*, 'God, I thank thee that I am not like other men, extortioners, unjust, adulterers, or even like this tax collector. I fast twice a week, I give tithes of all that I get' " (Luke 18:11–12).

The book of Proverbs says, "It is better to be an ordinary man working for a living than to play the part of a great man but go hungry. A good man takes care of his animals, but wicked men are cruel to theirs" (Prov. 12:9–10, TEV).

The competitive spirit runs amok in the self-absorbed person's disparagement of his or her neighbor. In the words of a contemporary psychoanalyst, Harry Stack Sullivan, "This disparagement business is really like the dust of the streets—it settles everywhere. . . . Since you have to protect your feeling of personal worth by noting how unworthy everybody around you is, you are not provided with any data that are convincing evidence of your having personal worth; so it gradually evolves into 'I am not as bad as other swine' " (Sullivan 1953: 242).

But the apostle Paul's wisdom offers the antidote to self-absorption and disparagement in a description of the productive and creative expression of competition: "Let love be genuine; . . . love one another with brotherly affection; outdo one another in showing honor" (Rom. 12:9).

Experimenting in Empathy for the Self-Absorbed Person

The whole exercise of developing a behavioral profile or description of the self-centered, narcissistic person may prompt you and me to disparage these persons and to thank God we are not like them. If your emotions have been pulled as mine have, you may sometimes feel that you are looking into a mirror at yourself. These persons test one's patience and very quickly shorten the fuses of psychiatrists, social workers, psychologists, and pastoral counselors alike. The reason for this is that they are resistant to insight-release kinds of therapy, and psychiatric medications are only transiently applicable and helpful; it is unimaginable that a narcissistic person would come presenting self-absorption as his or her chief complaint. These characters ought to be dealt with! Yet professionals who have clinical responsibility for them—teachers, pastors of churches, professors in colleges and professional schools—have natural, longer-term interaction with them in their contexts. How can *we* outdo these persons in honor?

Their Spiritual Legacy

One way is to school ourselves in learning their spiritual legacy. How did they get this way?

One root among many roots of self-absorbed persons' spiritual legacy is their feeling from very early in life that their care givers could not be depended on. When they were quite young, the verbal or nonverbal message they got was, "If you get taken care of, you are going to have to do it yourself!" They learned that their care givers did not willingly and lovingly do anything for them. They became survivalists, and survival was achieved by forcing or manipulating others to do what they needed and wanted. These skills became second nature to them, knee-jerk reactions. In adulthood, manipulation ceased to be for survival and became a "cleverness" manipulation. Their arrogance was finely honed by the time they reached their late teens.

These persons rarely seek pastoral counseling or psychiatric treatment except in the crisis of a severe job loss, a death, the breakup of a marriage. Remarkably enough, these griefs are the "teachable moments" when the church and its ministry appropriately takes the initiative. These persons, however, give off such an air of self-sufficiency that the ordinary ministries are not instituted, because "they can take care of themselves." In other words, we continue the message they got from their earliest spiritual legacy. In between such crises, too, narcissistic personalities may have alienated so many of the fellowship of faith and their co-workers on the job that hostility dictates such nonverbal thoughts as "let them stew in their own juice for a while. It'll do them good!" Thus we continue the old messages.

A far more compassionate and empathic approach is not to let these persons sell you a bill of goods about their marvelous self-sufficiency. It is better to treat them as we would anyone else in their plight. We can ambush them with surprise by "seeing past" their arrogance to find a person trying to wring out of us what he or she has already assumed we were not willing to do. The best way to throw such manipulative operators off balance is to outdo them with the same kind of honor we would like to receive ourselves. This may not change their basic life-style, but it puts it out of operation as far as we are concerned.

Another possible root in the spiritual heritage of these persons is not rejection, abandonment, and disillusionment, although it may be a "sweeter" form of these. That root is parental overvaluation and indulgence. Sigmund Freud describes this in vivid detail (1914:48):

> [Parents] are impelled to ascribe to the child all manner of perfections which sober observations would not confirm, to gloss over and forget all his shortcomings. . . . Moreover, they are inclined to suspend in the child's favor all those cultural requirements which their own narcissism has been forced to renew and respect, and to renew in his person the claims for the privileges which were long ago given up by themselves. [The child] is really to be the center and heart of creation.

What this kind of Little Lord Fauntleroy or Daddy's Little Girl treatment from doting parents does is to leave children without an internal gyroscope to guide them with realistic self-appraisals as they interact with other people. Putting them on a pedestal trains them to be a little god or goddess without flaw. They enter the world outside the home with a sense of entitlement and without the education in reasonable amounts of frustration which the world presents without trying to be difficult.

As pastors and as teachers at all levels, including college and professional school, we meet these "exceptional" persons. They may in fact have superior intelligence, and some may have been "born with a silver spoon in their mouth." We may be prone to continue the pattern of overrating them in response to their seductive manipulations to maneuver themselves into exemption from the ordinary demands of academic productivity. To treat them with honor in the same way we treat other people challenges their spiritual heritage. To involve them in small-group interactions with other students in which the response of peers is a frank but considerate self-appraisal process provides an access to self-absorbed persons that rarely if ever occurs in a psychiatric setting. When these persons do go for therapeutic help, they are usually in deep trouble of some kind and facing a serious loss.

In these group interactions, William Reid (1983:190–191) says that the goals are to help the person develop healthy individuality that does not need so much "resilient narcissism." A group will naturally challenge the self-defeating coping mechanisms of narcissistic persons. This will surprise and hurt them, but the group leader can enter into their world with empathy and thus affirm their right to such feelings. The client-centered teaching of Carl Rogers provides a helpful model for teaching such persons in a small group. He suggests a facilitative approach to being a leader that is helpful with narcissistic members of the group. The attitude of puzzlement that encourages the rather global statements of the person to be more carefully honed is helpful. I saw one teacher help such a person, who entered the class in the middle of the year as a transfer student. She quite privately after class affirmed the strongest point in what the student had to say. Then, almost as an afterthought, she added, "Being new here will take some getting used to and that will take time. I'll be here. You can count on me when it gets spooky." She understood that his insides were shaking behind his mask of cockiness.

Someone has said that it is easier for a good teacher, pastor, or counselor to tame a wild horse than resurrect a dead one. Narcissists are bundles of creativity that need taming. They are a challenge, but it takes an inner awareness that they frankly say about themselves what others carry as their secrets. We can thank God for a certain naïveté and guilelessness in them. That is a rare metal in the human spirit. But it has to be mined and refined over a period of time by gentle nudgings and confrontations. If we do not write them off or give up on them, they just may learn (1) that we can be counted on through thick and thin and (2) that if anybody is going to break the relationship between us, they will have to do it.

4

The Mask
of Hostility and Aggression

The American culture in which we have grown up and are now living has an unwritten but powerful set of expectations and demands for certain dimensions of each of the personality disorders we have discussed thus far. The antisocial, hostile-aggressive way of life seems most in demand. We have wildfires of popular hysteria for heroes, and there is widespread hero worship of movie actors and actresses. To stand up where it would count and challenge this hero worship would be to invite violent attack by mobs of devotees. The recent observance of the birthday of Elvis Presley would be such an occasion. Sylvester Stallone's Rambo, the hyperaggressive superpatriot movie character, glorifies many of the characteristics of the hostile-aggressive way of life we are about to discuss. The Old West–John Wayne syndrome is another case in point. "Dirty Dozens" of these hostile-aggressive role models are generated by the media. As soon as one loses box office appeal, decides to make a living some other way, or dies of an accident, a drug overdose, or old age, another takes his or her place.

The research and reflections of psychiatrists about the hostile-aggressive way of life show the influence of these pantheons of hostile-aggressive people too. Theodore Millon takes issue forthrightly with what he calls the DSM "label" of "antisocial," because it places "too great an emphasis on the delinquent, criminal, and other undesirable social consequences" often found among persons of a hyperaggressive life-style. He considers the DSM description of this disorder to be regressive in that only minor changes are made in earlier labeling of these persons as suffering from "constitutional psychopathic inferiority," "moral insanity," "criminal insanity," "psychopathic deviance," and so on (Millon 1981·181). However, the criminal elements of this population are the ones who—often in handcuffs and leg chains—are literally brought to the psychiatrist's attention. Psychiatric interpretation and theory tend to be built on populations whom the psychiatrists encounter clinically.

Nevertheless, I heartily agree with Millon's reaction. I hope that in the revision of DSM III now in progress his important observation will have some real effect. Millon (1981:182) further clarifies his objection:

> Only a minor subset of the aggressive personality pattern comes into conflict with the law. Many find themselves commended and reinforced in our competitive society where tough, hard-headed "realism" is admired as an attribute necessary for survival. Most find a socially valuable niche in the rugged side of the business, military, political [and, I would add, ecclesiastical] world. Their behaviors are seen in arrogant "patriotism" of nationalists whose truculence is "justified" by the hostility of "alien" groups. Such behavior is evident also in the machinations of politicians whose facade of good intentions cloaks a lust for power that leads to repressive legislation. Less dramatically, and more frequently, these individuals participate in the ordinary affairs of everyday life: the harsh, punitive father; the puritanical, fear-inducing minister; the vengeful dean; the irritable, guilt-producing mother.

I might add that in what Arnold S. Relman, editor of the *New England Journal of Medicine,* calls the recent "medical-industrial complex" (1980:963), hostile-aggressive personalities have new frontiers of an "Old West" to be a law unto themselves. The medical-industrial complex referred to by Relman is the large hospital–hospital supplies–hospital insurance conglomerates who are aggressively buying doctors' practices, stamping out or taking over competitors, and hogging the market in opposition to the independent physician or nonprofit hospital. He says—and I have observed—that these corporate giants skim the cream of the available patients. They take the most routine and those who are easily cared for in a short time and *not* the difficult-to-treat patients with a poor prognosis. Financially helpless individuals, such as some children, elderly persons, and psychiatric patients, are not taken. They are left to philanthropic and government-supported medical facilities.

We denizens of the life of the churches, then, are a part of this land of ours that spawns, employs, and applauds *some* of the "antisocial" or "hostile-aggressive" personality disorders to which we are giving our undivided attention.

Some Major Features of the Hostile-Aggressive Way of Life

A Plunging, Impulsive Initiative

Hostile-aggressive persons fear nothing and plunge undaunted into activities that more observant and reserved persons would accurately assess as dangerous. The punishing consequences of their actions do not deter them from further headstrong lunges. They are warlike in their attempts at the solution of almost any problem. They are like James and John, disciples of Jesus whom he named Boanerges, "sons of thunder." Their response to inhospitable Samaritans was to ask permission to call down fire from heaven and destroy them! (See Mark 3:17 and Luke 9:51–56.) One clue to dealing with such persons is having the courage that Jesus demonstrated to call their hand, to rebuke James and John without hesitation, and immediately to provide a more sensible answer. He did not equivocate with them, tremble at their rage, or haggle in indecision. Jesus and the disciples went on to another, more hospitable village.

An Overconfident and Inappropriately Assertive Self-Image

Hostile-aggressive persons place high value on being tough, thick-skinned, and powerful. They portray themselves as self-reliant, high-energy, and hardheaded. Intimidation is their tool of first choice in human relationships. They major in having other people fear them. You would readily identify this as a macho type of man or a butch kind of woman. In the contemporary and important struggle of women to become more assertive and less compliant, this brash, arrogant, and resentful life-style occasionally becomes another maladaptive alternative for women. Assertiveness need not be this maladaptive, nor are women without better alternatives than the more unsavory behaviors of men. This is to say, however, that just as the histrionic way of life is not restricted to women, the hostile-aggressive way of life is not restricted to men.

Combativeness and a Belligerent Attitude

DSM III lays great emphasis upon the recklessness and fighting behavior of the antisocial or hostile-aggressive person. Sociological data about the social class of the person qualifies this. Combativeness and belligerence pick up the tools that are available. People who live and work in a hard-hat arena or play football or hockey for a living may use fists and weapons. People who live and work in an academic or a hospital environment may use the bureaucratic process of committees, boards, and the like to express their combativeness and belligerence. People raised on or surviving on the streets may use vandalism, theft, and drugs as tools of combativeness and belligerence. People who go to church and have positions in the leadership of congregations and denominational hierarchies may use their powers of debate, exclusion and inclusion, and theological name-calling to express their belligerence and combativeness. All of them love a fight. If there is not one going, they will start one! Many churches have at least one such person who "was born in the objective case and the kickative mood."

In the home, moreover, verbal abuse and physical abuse erupt when the low frustration tolerance of the hostile-aggressive person is even slightly tested. Little children, particularly, live in fear of these persons, whether mother or father or both.

Interpersonal Vindictiveness

Hostile-aggressive personalities are not given to "being hurt" and falling into tears. They are given to vengeance. As some say, "I don't get angry. I get even." In its more refined forms, this vindictiveness appears under a social mask. They may appear to be very suave, sincere, and "adult." They are not troubled by a sense of guilt, but only comforted in making someone pay for what they do not like. They may quietly form their "enemies lists." With considerable glee and cleverness they lay a trap for the person with whom they are trying to settle the score. As the psalmist says,

> Those who seek my life lay their snares,
> those who seek my hurt speak of ruin,
> and meditate treachery all the day long.
> (Psalm 38:12)

This dimension of the hostile-aggressive way of life is acted out monotonously in the character of J. R. Ewing in the television soap opera *Dallas.* People *enjoy* hating him! The secular wisdom of professional politics is not code enough for the hostile-aggressive person's lack of foresight. It is an unwritten law of effective statesmanship that magnanimity or greatness of heart toward one's opponent is the most effective way of swaying votes of reasonable people.

The important missing element in the hostile-aggressive life-style, however, is that such magnanimity calls for foresight. These persons don't have it. They are "short-term greedy," with a low frustration tolerance if they don't get what they want immediately. As Proverbs 12:11 puts it, "A hard-working farmer has plenty to eat, but it is stupid to waste time on useless projects" (TEV). "Stupid" here does not mean the *lack* of intelligence, but the refusal of the unteachable to *use* the intelligence God has given them.

A Cynical View of Other People

The psalmist acknowledged, "I said in my haste, all men are liars" (Ps. 116:11, KJV)—or, "I said in my consternation, 'Men are all a vain hope' " (RSV). However you translate it, this is the theme of the hostile-aggressive person. DSM III says that such a person "claims that most people are devious and punitive" and "justifies his or her own mistrustful, hostile, and vengeful attitudes by ascribing them to others." Other persons are not to be trusted until they have proven themselves to be loyal. The basic trust that Erikson considers the foundation of emotional maturity gives way in the antisocial personality to a self-sufficient justification of ruthlessness.

Amoral Ruthlessness in the Acquisition of Power

The absence of a moral code in these personalities has caused many observers to think of them as "morally diseased." But this is a metaphorical use of the word "disease" that is misleading. From the overview of Jewish and Christian wisdom literature, this is not a disease as much as it is a profligate misuse of intelligence. It is "smart" stupidity in which a person will tell a lie when the truth would do better. It is selling one's soul for a mess of pottage. In order to get immediate satisfaction of a fleeting desire, hostile-aggressive persons will compromise long-term investments of life and its resources for short-term success and demonstration of personal power. They want all the power and glory of all the kingdoms of this world "in a moment of time" (see Luke 4:5–6). As one ecclesiastical power figure put it, "I know all the people who work for me like my hand. I know exactly how much power each one of them has, and what it will take to take that power from them!" The irony is that he himself did not pay any of their salaries! Money was given in freewill offerings by Christian donors. Structurally, people did not work *for* him but *with* him. Only he seemed not to know this!

I have said that these people are amoral. They are so in the sense that the main ingredients of a mutual social covenant or contract between them and those to whom they are related is inoperative. They are callous to it. As Jean Jacques Rousseau stated that social contract, "The problem is to find a form of association which will defend and protect with the whole common force the person and goods of each associate, and in which each, while uniting himself with all, may still obey himself alone, and remain as free as before." The term "antisocial" is an accurate portrayal of persons for whom such a social contract is null and void. They live for personal power and control over the whole social scene they survey.

Manipulation and coercion become the tools of conquest for antisocial persons. If acting gracious, cheerful, and charming will maneuver and subjugate, that is the way to go. If such behavior fails, frustration of their will to power easily turns into furious, vindictive attacks. The people and institutions around them become tools of power. Religion and its pieties are subordinated to the iron necessities of their personal need to control. Here the antisocial and narcissistic ways of life flow into each other and are hardly distinguishable.

Status Consciousness

One important dimension of hostile-aggressive personalities is rarely mentioned in the psychiatric literature. Neither DSM III nor Millon call attention to their status consciousness. They exist in the prestige dimension of human life that stratifies their world, separating it into different levels or degrees of class, status, and power. The religious community is no exception, but rather an example of such status levels of prestige-seeking. The dream of a classless society evaporates in the heat of the accumulation of power. Antisocial persons may be cynically ingratiating, cooperative, and seemingly unselfish as they move up the ladder of the power structure. As one psychologist put it, however, they will inveterately "kiss those above them and kick those below them." When they have arrived at the pinnacle of their particular temple, they are in the world to be ministered unto by all those beneath them. They spend their time, energy, and attention in feathering their own nest and maintaining their position of power.

In order to *stay* in power and on top, they surround themselves with a palace guard that protects them from and in-
forms them about those whom they distrust, who are hostile,
whom they should punish, and upon whom they would visit
vengeance. The tragedy of their lives is, as the former president of Harvard University, Dr. Nathan Pusey, once told a
group of which I was a member, "The members of their own
palace guard are the ones who finally destroy them, as was
true of Julius Caesar."

In the person of Jesus Christ, we know that there are other
constructive expressions of power and influence. The hostile-
aggressive way happens to be the maladaptive expression of
hostile-aggressive, antisocial personalities. Their leadership
is a mask covering a war on both society and sanity.

Bases of Empathy
for the Hostile-Aggressive Personality

A person's life story provides some understanding of the
inner world of the antisocial personality. The first and most
prevalent impression you get is that this person has suffered
parental rejection, discontent, and hostility. This may well
have been compounded by teachers who responded in a
similar manner. Such rejection may come from many
sources of which the child has no real awareness—an un-
wanted pregnancy, severe occupational and financial difficulties, rage toward a spouse. Roughshod and inconsiderate
behavior toward the child is not only a rejection but an example—one of the few the child has—to copy. Even a newborn infant in an atmosphere of sustained hostility and ag-
gression gets the feeling that the world is an unfriendly,
threat-filled place. Wariness and distrust become second nature. The initial groundwork of these persons is not anger
and hostility but fear—nameless, terror-producing, and awe-
some.

Such rejection, hostility, and discontent with a child can
infiltrate a whole family who live in a milieu of a "siege mentality." Members of a hated, despised, and abused minority
such as Jews, blacks, Chicanos, and others are examples of
this. The early life of Sigmund Freud was beset by such events
as his father being pushed into the ditch from the sidewalk,
and his having been denied educational funds because he was
a Jew. His dreams in later life reflect his rage toward the pope
and other Christians who meted out this treatment. Robert
Coles quotes a ten-year-old black child:

> Keep your fear of the white man,
> my momma tells each of us
> all the time until
> we know it for ourselves.
> Be afraid, be scared of being
> curious, if you want to know
> too much about them
> you'll step too far,
> you'll overstep.
> Know to be afraid.

Another such siege mentality is that of dispossessed and poverty-stricken populations. Whole families of sharecroppers, sporadically employed miners, mill workers, and "surplus" youth live in a world they perceive as "devious, controlling, and punitive," to repeat DSM III's description of the antisocial personality. No accounting of the upbringing of these persons can eliminate such social sources of rage. Yet a puzzling question arises as to the factors that, under the same conditions, make for persons with a keen sense of personal and social injustice, and at the same time produce amoral, socially callous persons such as the hostile-aggressive and antisocial person. My own hypothesis is that a grandmother or grandfather, an older sibling, a neighbor, a pastor, or a teacher very early supplied an unconditional love, a balanced sense of humor, and teachability to the individual who turned out differently. Also, I am convinced that personality is never completely "made." Persons in adolescence or early and even middle maturity have spiritual transformations that turn them around, change their directions, and hitch their rage to the creative purposes of God for their lives. This happens neither as often as the churches would like us to believe nor as seldom as the behavioral sciences tend to assume. But it does happen in situations such as that of Augustine, Malcolm X, Charles Colson, and lesser lights like myself. Rage is to the human organism as fire is to human life. It can destroy or heat, warm, cook, and create tremendous human strength. The major issue is its control and the kind of intelligence, understanding, and foresight that guides its use.

Another genesis of antisocial or hostile aggressive lifestyles appears in adolescence. Without adequate adult models for ethically channeling the aggressions of the child, the next best opportunity for this is a grafting of the ethical sensitivity of another family through a close chum of a similar age and the same sex. During this relatively brief era, the child sees a different model from that of his or her nuclear family in a

cousin, a neighbor, or a schoolmate from across town or
across the county. He or she gets a new pattern to go by. Also,
this person may come from another milieu than one of a siege
mentality. A black child meets a white child and they build a
world of their own, unbeknown to either set of parents. A
Jewish child and a Christian child each learn that the other is
human, to be trusted, and they begin to work easily together.

If something like this does not happen in early childhood
or preadolescence, the child grows into adolescence. The
peer group itself becomes the source of authority. If this peer
group is composed solely of hostile, suspicious, and cynical
members, then the adult world becomes the stupid, not-to-
be-trusted, punishing world. This becomes the training
ground for the kind of life-style we have been discussing.
They become imprisoned in a culture of "rebels without a
cause," trouble on its way to happening.

The importance of a group to a hostile-aggressive individual points to the usefulness of teaching, activities, sports, and
therapeutic groups as mediums of care and confrontation.
Likewise, if you as the group leader can be realistic but kind
and accepting toward these individuals, asking them to see
you personally after a group meeting if they become too explosive, you will start them on the road toward self-individua-
tion apart from a group, a gang, or an audience. If ever once
they can function apart from pack thinking, they may begin to
like themselves and other people better.

Another source of empathy for aggressive-hostile persons
is to look at the other side of their aggressive pushiness that
ignores the personal space or territory of other people. The
other side of it is oversensitivity to people trying to "get too
close" to them. Their "taboo on tenderness" reflects the fear
of losing their own personal space, their own "territory." The
territorial imperative is almost a given with these persons.
You can be aware of this and quietly maintain a distinct territory of your own. An evenly hovering attentiveness filled with
much listening to brash statements until they begin to hear
themselves talk is the best way to go. Proverbs 15:1–2 puts it
best: "A soft answer turns away wrath, but a harsh word stirs
up anger." Also, James 1:19 conveys the essence of skill in
relating to the hostile-aggressive person: "Let every man be
quick to hear, slow to speak, slow to anger."

A large part of maintaining your separateness as a person
in your own right lies in brevity, clarity, and directness of
speech when such a person seeks to manipulate you. Jesus
warned, "Let what you say be simply 'Yes' or 'No'; anything

more than this comes from evil" (Matt. 5:37). The manipulative attempts of hostile-aggressive persons spring from their tacit assumption that they are clever and you are stupid. A frank, direct, unequivocal no tells them that you will not be maneuvered, manipulated, or used. Jesus' injunction to be wise as a serpent and guileless or harmless as a dove is apropos. Strong sales resistance and a refusal to be frightened by threats turn you, who had been assumed to be an easy prey, into at least an object of curiosity and maybe even a challenge. They are accustomed to being rejected outright, not being resisted with gentleness and evenhanded good humor.

Basic Spiritual Challenges of the Hostile-Aggressive

The stewardship of anger, the "acceptance of acceptance," a spiritual transformation of power focus from the self to God, a discovery of teachability, and the discipline of considerateness are critical spiritual challenges confronting the hostile-aggressive person. Your and my chances to begin such a dialogue with them usually come when these persons' way of life has disappointed or defeated them. This may be in their work, in their family life, in their severe loss of something or someone useful to them, or when they are severely embarrassed or humiliated. At these times they can become reactively depressed. From a pastoral point of view, this depression is a complicated grief state. Older persons among them are facing existential issues of heart attacks, the shortness of the life ahead of them, and the fact that all personal empires tend to dissolve when younger competitors make a move to take over. Mandatory retirement presents them with propositions they can't refuse. So much of the antisocial way of life depends upon an abundance of energy and excellent physical health.

When life itself begins to close in on hostile-aggressive persons, pastoral access to them becomes easier. You and I need not count on this too heavily, because when an immediate crisis is over, or as it could be said less elegantly, "when they get their tail out of a pinching crack," they tend not to need us any more. We do what we can when the heat is on.

The Stewardship of Anger

The anger of the hostile-aggressive person wreaks havoc. It is passed on in a family from one generation to another. A good way of looking at it is as "runaway creativity." The teachings of Jesus and Paul make it clear that anger is not evil in itself. However, as with any other endowment of the human creation, such as intelligence, it can be a liability that brings us into judgment. Our great gifts are at the same time our path to destruction if they are not under the control of the intentions, purpose, and spiritual presence of God. Thus controlled, they become redemptive rather than destructive, creative rather than debilitating. The "sons of thunder," James and John, started out with Jesus as "hawks," depending on their own equivalent of nuclear power. When they had been taught by Jesus, tradition tells us, James became the arbiter of conflict in the Jerusalem church; John became the mystic seer of the Apocalypse.

The warlike spirit of antisocial persons needs, as William James put it, a "moral equivalent of war." They are in rebellion against early rejections. All this energy calls for stewardship in a higher calling than "looking out for Number One," self-aggrandizement, and manipulation of other people. If you have a group of adolescents or a group of young couples who work in the business world, a helpful exploration of the stewardship of anger could be a gentle way of dealing with these personality life-styles in the group. For a guide, use the book by Andrew D. Lester, *Coping with Your Anger: A Christian Guide.* You will have a lively time of it. How can all this anger be dedicated to God's service without the cleverness, manipulation, and contempt for other people?

Of course such a group discussion, from the leader's point of view, would bring out the deeper concerns behind the anger: our early feelings of rejection, our basic fear and distrust of the dependability of other people, our self-sufficiency.

The "Acceptance of Acceptance"

The age-old contention of hostile-aggressive persons is that they are rejected by others, and the derived assumption is that other people cannot be trusted, depended upon, or believed. To meet someone—or Someone, in the person of Jesus Christ—who *is* trustworthy, can be depended upon, and whose word is true can shake the foundations of a hostile-aggressive person. God is at work for the "removal of what is shaken, as of what has been made, in order that what cannot be shaken may remain," says Hebrews 12:27. For God to "shake" the created structure of rejection in these persons' lives is our prayer. For them to meet someone in you or me or a group of which we are a part who genuinely accepts them is a shaking event. For you or me and our group to see through their brashness, arrogance, and manipulativeness and find a scared, terror-stricken, unloved and unlovable person shatters their presuppositions about life.

To do this is to accept such persons as they are behind their masks. Then their task is to accept the acceptance. Their first thought with regard to us who would accept them is, "They are not real. They've got an angle. They are getting something out of this. Everybody's got a racket. I'll stick around out of curiosity to see what it is!" Then our acceptance is put to the test. Is it our effort to manipulate them, to get new members in our church, to get their money for our projects, to make a good attendance showing in the church school enlargement contest, or what?

Or is our one concern that these persons know God in Jesus Christ, who has a place for sons or daughters of thunder in his new order of human life? He has a grace and an acceptance, an unfathomable understanding of the rejected, feverishly cocksure person. As Paul Tillich says, faith in God's love means that we can accept being accepted though we know we are unacceptable. To be forgiven and to believe it is a plainer way of saying it.

The Transformation of the Power Focus from the Self to God

The crucial spiritual concern with aggressive-hostile persons is their ingrained tendency to focus on themselves the power, status, and control in any relationship. When one of the traumatic events of life hits them, they find themselves, as Elijah did, in their own particular wilderness of the spirit. They are likely to feel, as he did, "I, even I only, am left; and they seek my life, to take it away" (1 Kings 19:10). God made his presence known as a power greater than Elijah's, and gave Elijah some humbling news: You are not alone; there are seven thousand others who have not bowed the knee to Baal or kissed him. Thus Elijah's hostile, warlike centering of power in himself was shaken and a new order of his life came into being.

I have seen this kind of transformation dramatically take place in a few antisocial personalities whom I have served. We have autobiographical accounts of such events in the stories of persons like Malcolm X and Charles Colson. Colson describes himself in the language of this chapter; he was "the outstanding young man of Boston . . . , clawing and straining for status and position." He speaks of his "arrogance over an enemy brought to submission" (1967:114).

During his severe loss and humiliation, and before his imprisonment, Charles Colson visited a friend of his, Tom Phillips, who

> was so gentle I couldn't resent what he said as he cut right through it all: "Chuck, I hate to say this, but you guys [in the Watergate scandal] brought it on yourselves. If you had put your faith in God, and if your cause were just, He would have guided you. . . . Chuck, I don't think you will understand what I'm saying about God until you are willing to face yourself honestly and squarely. This is the first step." (Colson 1976: 112)

They read through one chapter of C. S. Lewis's *Mere Christianity* on human pride as the chief misery of life. After more extended conversation, Colson permitted Phillips to pray with him. He was shaken deeply but thanked his host and left. He drove his car a few hundred yards from Phillips' house but was so upset that he pulled over and parked.

> With my face cupped in my hands, head leaning forward against the wheel, I forgot about machoism, about pretenses, about fears of being weak. And as I did, I began to experience a wonderful feeling of being released. Then came the strange sensation that water was not only running down my cheeks, but surging through my whole body as well, cleansing and cooling as it went. They weren't tears of sadness and remorse, nor of joy—but somehow, tears of relief.
>
> And then I prayed my first real prayer. "God, I don't know how to find You, but I'm going to try! I'm not much the way I am now, but somehow I want to give myself to You." I didn't know how to say more, so I repeated over and over the words: *Take me. . . .* That night, something inside me was urging me to surrender—to what or to whom I did not know.
>
> I stayed there in the car, wet-eyed, praying, thinking, for perhaps half an hour, perhaps longer, alone in the quiet of the dark night. Yet for the first time in my life I was not alone at all. (Colson 1976:116–117)

Colson took off his mask. The focus of power was being shifted from him as a power figure to God. Something inside him was urging him to surrender.

Harry M. Tiebout speaks of an "act of surrender" in persons addicted to alcohol. The addiction can as easily be to power and the enchantment of our own cleverness. In defining this act of surrender he says (1950:1), "It is to be viewed as a moment when the unconscious forces of defiance and grandiosity actually cease to function effectively. When that happens, the individual is wide open to reality; he can listen and learn without fighting back."

You can readily see that the result of this act of surrender, this shifting of the focus of power from the self to God, is the ability to listen and learn. Colson gave up his assumption that he knew it all and that no one could teach him anything. Reverence for the power of God and the capacity to listen and learn are all the fruits of the Spirit in the life of a hostile-aggressive person. As a result of their capacity to listen and learn is the discovery that some people can be trusted, and that those people's judgment, input, and fellowship are indispensable to their new being in God. Gone is the cocksure cleverness, and in its place is a new gentleness and considerateness.

The Disciplines of Considerateness

The harsh verbal and sometimes physical abuse that hostile-aggressive persons dish out presents them with a long pilgrimage in laying aside their ruthlessness, vengefulness, and even brutality to others. Certainly their heartlessness in delighting to make defenseless people squirm with humiliation calls for a new lifelong discipline of considerateness. Gentleness can be learned. Colson noted that Phillips, though he was president of a large corporation, was *gentle.* One of the fruits of the spirit is gentleness (Gal. 5:22). Another gift is self-control. These gifts of the Spirit atrophy if they are not exercised. As such they are disciplines, especially for the hostile-aggressive person who was taught to be tough and to interpret gentleness as either stupid or weak.

The best place to start the exercise of gentleness and considerateness is with little children. In anger we are to be as children. They do not let the sun go down on their wrath. It is only from older persons that children learn how to carry a grudge, how to plan to get even, and how to be vindictive. In our own demeanor with hostile-aggressive persons, gentleness is our greatest strength. It confuses them because it is a different pattern of living. It may even intrigue them. As the Taoist proverb puts it, "He who is genuinely strong has no fear of being gentle."

5

The Mask
of Passive Aggression

Whereas hostile-aggressive persons are obsessed with *capturing* power and authority, passive-aggressive persons are not obsessed with *having* power. They are beset with the temptation to resist authority. Millon speaks of them as oppositional or negativistic personalities. Many ambivalent and contradictory behaviors take place. At one time the person will be dependently compliant and later will be inappropriately assertive and independent. "Mr. Facing-Both-Ways" is the name John Bunyan would have given this person. A chronic discontent pervades this person's existence.

A Profile of the Passive-Aggressive Way of Life

Passive Resistance to Demands for Performance

The high school, college, seminary, or medical student resists the authority of the system by not attending class, by turning in late papers, by requesting makeup exams, and by asking to be given an "incomplete" at the end of a term in which he or she has done little work.

The passive-aggressive person will come to an agreement with his or her spouse that a certain thing will be done but will procrastinate and never get around to it. The other spouse will use reminders, then nag, then become more intense, and finally explode in anger. The passive-aggressive partner then is hurt, does not talk much, sulks, and pouts.

At church a passive-aggressive who is chosen to chair a committee may never get around to having meetings of the group, and when deadlines for reports or actions are at hand he or she is not ready.

On the job, passive-aggressive persons may function very well if they do not have any major responsibility, but they may be sloppy in making decisions and implementing them. This is because decision-making and implementation are done within definite spaces of time. I have observed that passive-aggressive persons seem to live in a timeless world of their own. Calendars, clocks, and watches have little meaning to them.

Also, people now in their thirties and early forties grew up in the Vietnam era and may have been affected by the hippie counterculture. One of the legacies we have of that era is the "laid-back" person. The timeless consciousness was then said to be one hallmark of "Consciousness III" folk in the Now Generation. People who were young adults during that era were also subject to being drafted for the Vietnam War. They were not given the right to plan their own lives. Many seemed to be saying, "You do what you feel like in the intensity of the present. You don't program yourself with timetables, schedules, deadlines, etc. No matter what you plan, you will mess up." Thus passive resistance to authority is a characteristic traceable to a cultural revolution as well as a given upbringing in a particular family (see Reich 1970: 217–263).

Specific Passive-Aggressive Behaviors

A quintet of passive-aggressive behaviors are the almost automatic, knee-jerk responses of the passive-aggressive person's resistance to authority, to the ordinary demands of people who are responsible for seeing to it that the day-to-day business of a home, a job, or a school gets done: procrastination, dawdling, stubbornness, intentional inefficiency, and forgetfulness.

These five behaviors are commonly listed as diagnostic criteria. I would add: (1) a time awareness that focuses on the present moment and deletes memory of past mistakes, ignoring the foresight called for in planning, calculating risks, and being ready for either opportunities or upcoming threats to one's best interests, and (2) a passive refusal to accept the instruction, discipline, and sacrifice involved in earning credentials for getting ahead in a culture that values greatly such things as high school diplomas, college degrees, professional competency certifications and licenses, and labor union membership.

Chronic and Long-Term Ineffectiveness in Job and Marital and Family Responsibilities

This includes responsibilities like getting an adequate and satisfying job, functioning well as a student, and doing the things that will merit promotion. While the power-driven hostile-aggressive person will manipulate and orchestrate in any power structure in order to get ahead, the passive-aggressive person will do the minimum to get by and, more or less intentionally, is inefficient about doing the things necessary to get ahead. My observation of those I counsel reveals a large number of persons with this life-style who say they want to be in business for themselves. They want to be writers, but they avoid the disciplines of sustained use of time in writing and in many instances do not want to study English composition and literature; they don't even read much. They want to be business persons, but they are not willing to learn business administration, cost accounting, maintaining cash flow, and the like. They want to be landscape specialists, but they are not interested in studying horticulture. They want to be builders, but they don't want to learn about contracts, deeds, architecture, engineering. They want to "make it big" as musicians, but they don't want to study with a professional music teacher. They feel that they can pick up these things from experience, on their own.

Unwillingness to Choose a Teacher

Several months ago I attended a Bar Mitzvah for a colleague's son. The rabbi, in his charge to the young man, quoted from the Talmud three "necessities for living effectively among the people of the earth": "First, choose yourself a teacher and follow your teacher's instructions as a good disciple. Second, choose yourself a friend from whom you can learn and with whom you can work. Third, judge people on their own merits without letting what you hear about them determine your thoughts."

One of the major difficulties in persons with a passive-aggressive personality is their unwillingness to choose a teacher and a friend from whom they can learn a discipline and how to practice it. They are willing to accept money and other favors from persons in authority, but they are unwilling to accept consultation, instruction, warning, or admonition.

The Passive-Aggressive Person in Action

I Keep Waiting for My Big Chance

Whereas resisting authority seems to be a way of life for passive-aggressive persons, they seem to rely almost superstitiously on chance, the odds, fate. They carry a persistent mood of never having any luck. Their essential religion is one of luck, not Providence. The world withholds from them its silver and gold, and they are victimized. They are forced by circumstances to get along on meager fare. As Millon states it, life "has been unkind to them. They feel cheated and unappreciated. Whatever they have done is for naught" (1981:255). Their rationale for this is that they are just unlucky. Then again, in a specific situation where things did not turn out right, it was because other people let them down, did not do what they said they would do, or were plainly not doing their job right.

Greek mythology once again comes to our aid in understanding the negativistic, passive-aggressive person in action. The Greeks had a trio of goddesses, the Fates, who determined life. Clotho spun the thread of a person's life. Lachesis, the disposer of lots or situations in life, determined the length of a person's life. Atropos, the inflexible, cut life off, put an end to it. Passive-aggressive persons seem locked into an unspoken belief that it is their lot to be losers. The thread of their life as it spins out is their evidence. They feel that they never seem to get anywhere. Quite in contrast to the competitive spirit of narcissistic and antisocial personalities, they drop out of any competition. They have a reverse snobbism about status and getting ahead in the world. If a pigeon flies over any crowd they are in, they are the one person upon whom the pigeon's droppings inevitably land!

These persons decry their situation in life and are quite vocal in describing their discontent. The desire to get at its roots and begin a program of changes to make life better is absent. When an approach to their situation is presented, they may courteously agree that it is a good strategy but will then say, "Yes, but . . ." and begin to point out all the hindrances they might encounter. Or they may quietly agree that these steps of action are to be taken. Then they procrastinate, dawdle, forget, and finally miss out on the opportunity because it is too late. In short, they let life pass by default. In not making a decision and not taking action, they have allowed life itself to make the decisions and take action to their disadvantage.

When this happens they become morose and sullen, and can be impulsive, unpredictable, and explosive. They make impulsive changes of jobs, spend money inordinately, or press their family into surprising and dramatic changes. In a rapid succession of changing behaviors and moods they say and do things, usually in the realm of money, jobs, and the buying or selling of property, that show great impairment of judgment.

I Really Don't Know What I Want to Do

The passive-aggressive character is a modern Hamlet. He or she constantly halts between the two sides of any impending decision.

> To be, or not to be: that is the question:
> Whether 'tis nobler in the mind to suffer
> The slings and arrows of outrageous fortune,
> Or to take arms against a sea of troubles,
> And by opposing end them?
>
> • • • • • • • • • • • • • • • • • •
>
> Thus conscience does make cowards of us all;
> And thus the native hue of resolution
> Is sicklied o'er with the pale cast of thought,
> And enterprises of great pith and moment
> With this regard their currents turn awry,
> And lose the name of action.
>
> (*Hamlet*, III, i, 56)

This indecision is seen in academia in the choice of a major in college, in the choice of a specialty in a professional school, and in the choice of a place to settle down after education is completed—if it ever is! The indecision shows itself in the nonverbal games that married couples play, never fully committing themselves to each other and yet not deciding to break up the marriage. All the while, these persons are alternately laden with feelings of guilt and feelings of resentment.

I Am Afraid I Will Make a Mistake

When one gets to know persons with a passive-aggressive life-style over a period of years, one notices how a strange sense of perfectionism emerges in the thoughts that they blurt out when under great anxiety. It usually is expressed as: "I am terrified that I will make a mistake!" They keep struggling with what Karen Horney called the "glorified self-image" of one who expects to make perfect decisions. With all their superstructure of being fated to bad luck, they carry a great deal of anxiety brought on by perfectionism. When they are under extreme pressure this can result in clinically manifest bodily symptoms—shortness of breath, constricted chest cavity, and heart-attack-like symptoms, for example. Medical intervention is highly appropriate. They are in real pain and deserve good medical care.

Avenues of Empathy for Passive-Aggressive Persons

Perfectionism and Fear of Making a Mistake

The perfectionism of passive-aggressive persons, with their ensuing procrastination and indecisiveness, is underneath much of their nonproductivity in school, work, and marital situations. They may suffer severe anxiety attacks at examination time or when an important paper is due. Those who are college teachers, knowing that promotion depends upon scholarly productivity, will agonize over writing an article or a book with the glorified image of themselves as writing a magnum opus worthy of national and international acclaim. But at the inner core of their being they carry much sweaty, unspeakable terror that they will make a mistake.

What are some of the origins of this? When you get them to recall when they first remember these feelings, you are likely to find that they had highly successful parents who expected perfection of themselves and demanded it of their sons and daughters. If they did not expect and demand it, the son or daughter *perceived* them as doing so. At one and the same time they felt guilty because their parents' expectation or example required this of them. Then they felt resentment because they needed to be loved no matter how badly they messed up. They began life with ambivalence of admiration and resentment for one or more parents who were a hard act to follow. This scenario is repeated again and again in clinical meetings with VIP parents who are perplexed and concerned about their underachieving sons or daughters. Again, culturally shaped attitudes toward "success" and "prestige" have something to do with the weaving of personalities such as those we are discussing here.

Having Lost the Parental Blessing

In a sense, the passive-aggressive person may have been positive and achieving in the earliest years of life. Such a person may have been an only child for several years before the next sibling was born. Then he or she was displaced by a younger brother or sister who did not tarry long about becoming the star performer of the family. The displaced first child then felt that the blessing of the parents had passed to the brother or sister, and thus gradually he or she turned from a creative, "sweet," articulate little child into a surly, negativistic young boy or girl. Such children do not feel safe about expressing directly and aggressively their feelings of injustice, loneliness, and hurt. Instead, they follow the hurtful course of procrastination, dawdling, low achievement, and nonproductivity. The younger child, being smaller and not knowing as much as the older one, does not make it any easier for this sullen older sibling. He or she actively *seeks* the blessing of the parents at the older sibling's expense. (For an excellent discussion of this, read Myron Madden's *The Power to Bless.*)

The Schismatic Family Atmosphere

Millon suggests from his research and clinical experience that the habitual passive-aggressive reaction to life can be the end result of being brought up by parents who are constantly demeaning each other and bickering with each other. He says that the children "are often forced to serve as mediators to moderate the tensions their parents generate. The children may be forced to switch sides and divide their loyalties from one moment to the next. They find that they are not free to be 'themselves' " (1981:267). The built-in ambivalence and indecisiveness of the passive-aggressive person's life may be mute testimony to this kind of history.

Allergy to the Responsibility of Becoming a Self in One's Own Right

These negativistic persons are "stuck" on the dark side of the moon of their own selfhood. Erik Erikson (1968:172–174) speaks of the choice of the negative identity:

> The loss of a sense of identity is often expressed in a scornful and snobbish hostility toward the roles offered as proper and

desirable in one's family or immediate community. . . . On the whole, however, our patients' conflicts find expression in a more subtle way than the abrogation of personal identity. They choose instead a *negative identity*, i.e., an identity based on all those identifications and roles which, at critical stages of development, had been presented to them as most undesirable or dangerous and yet also as most real.

These roles they have been warned against as being most undesirable and dangerous are often the roles that demand the least responsibility. Consequently, the young person can be interpreted by parents and more successful siblings as lazy, a dreamer, one of those who can never get their act together. Most people who know this person do not sense his or her despair or realize that such a person can become so guilt-ridden, anxiety-laden, and depressed as to be suicidal. Søren Kierkegaard has a profound grasp of this despair at becoming a self. He says, "Man is a synthesis of the finite and the infinite, of the temporal and the eternal, of freedom and necessity. . . . A synthesis is a relation between two factors. So regarded, man is not yet a self." Kierkegaard's assessment of the form of despair of negativistic, passive-aggressive persons is their despair at not being willing to be a self. All the options of identity are presented to them as a positive and creative call for discipline, self-sacrifice, and the acceptance of responsibility. They are allergic to all of these. They definitely refuse to become such a self. Yet the negative identity leaves them as vagabonds among those who love them, and they feel with their peers that they are part of a "lost generation" (Kierkegaard 1941:17).

Therefore, we tread softly with these persons. Our initial visceral response is to be put out with them, lose patience with them, and become angry at them. They are asking for this by the way they deal with us. In other words, we are being set up by them to break our relationship with them. They do not *plan* to do this; it just happens by "second nature." William H. Reid (1983:199) sagely warns, "Although [you] may feel angry . . . remember that the [person's] behavior, even if apparently voluntary, is defending against severe anxiety or deterioration."

Spiritual Dilemmas and Resources
of the Passive-Aggressive Personality

Unawareness of Time: Its Ends and End

When you become well acquainted with persons whose life pattern is passive-aggressive, you are struck with how they are unaware of time. In New Testament terms, they are not able to "discern the times," not aware of the "shortness of time." They fail to notice the impending end of each era of life and seem to be oblivious to the passing years. Hence, they do not work the works of Him who sent them while it is day, knowing that the time is coming when no one can work. Being "ready," therefore, is not a part of their conscious values and certainly not the tone and temper of their modes of existence. The sense of any sort of eschaton is absent. This spiritual cast of their lives hinders their basic function in every direction. Some will say that they listen to a different drummer, but when it comes to listening to the clock and the calendar and being aware of grace, they do not listen at all. Does this change and can it be changed?

It may change when they are massively disrupted and thrown off balance by the death of a person who has sponsored them and supported them when they were in trouble. If the passive-aggressive person happens to be alcoholic, this could be a parent, a spouse, or even a good friend who dies. The whole configuration of their stress system is thrown out of kilter. The reality of death and their own passing years may come home to them. Or, these supporting persons may finally say, "This has been going on long enough. It is at an end now." They quit loaning them money, no longer tiding them over chasms created by carelessness or lack of foresight. Parents will often ask, "How can I help this child?" The answer is, "Quit doing some of the things you are doing!" In Alcoholics Anonymous language this is called "raising the bottom" so that they will "hit bottom" sooner.

A narrow escape from death itself has a way of suddenly making the passive-aggressive person aware of the reality and value of time. Such a person may be suicide-prone. Suicide or an attempt at suicide *creates* the end. If a person fails in the attempt and this brings an awareness of how short and precious time is, then going to the edge of the abyss may create deep changes.

Yet life itself quite often does not present passive-aggressive persons with these traumas. Instead of being ready and prepared for the testing moments of life, they are like the foolish virgins who were unprepared for the master's return. Their lamps are empty and the wicks untrimmed. Instead, they may be *waiting* for an affluent parent to die, relying on their inheritance of the family fortune to justify their laid-back way of life. Their procrastination may have a covert venality fueled by their subtle death wish for the relative. This is a characteristic of well-to-do passive-aggressive people. They do not prepare for their own demise. They assume they will live forever. Yet they count on the death of affluent relatives.

If you and I are related to these persons as teachers, then the issue of time consciousness can be a part of the curriculum. A whole class can become a part of an experiment with time. I have had classes do a diary of their uses of time for the course of a week or a semester. I read these and not only learn much about how my students use their time but also am able to make concrete suggestions about how they might use it better.

If you and I are personal counselors of these persons, a good procedure is to raise the issue of time awareness, of which procrastination is only one expression, and to formulate a meaningful task that is to be completed in a certain length of time. Often these persons are job-hunting. The "homework" can be the preparation of a résumé of their educational and work history. A direct behavioral modification of the use of time can be a catalyst for larger personal changes.

Without some new perspective of time, the worldview of the negativistic, passive-aggressive person tends to coincide with Macbeth's pessimism:

> Tomorrow, and tomorrow, and tomorrow,
> Creeps in this petty pace from day to day,
> To the last syllable of recorded time;
> And all our yesterdays have lighted fools
> The way to dusty death. Out, out, brief candle!
> Life's but a walking shadow, a poor player
> That struts and frets his hour upon the stage,
> And then is heard no more; it is a tale
> Told by an idiot, full of sound and fury,
> Signifying nothing.
>
> (*Macbeth* V, v, 19)

An Impaired Capacity for Commitment
to a Clear Purpose

With a pessimism to match Macbeth's, the negativistic person has lost the self-confidence that is ordinarily replenished, renewed, and held steady in lean times by a clear sense of purpose. If life is a tale told by an idiot, signifying nothing, then people's hearts faint within them for lack of the passion of a purpose. At its most specific level, a passionate purpose centers around personal competence in a skill that you not only are trained and disciplined in but also enjoy. You don't just cook meals for a family; you are a diligent artist in the preparation of food that not only pleases the taste buds but is a creation of beauty appealing to the eye, the sense of smell, and even the sense of touch. You leave the fingerprints of your unique skill and inspired commitment to your task as a trademark of your positive identity in your world. Whatever you do, from the most basic manual task to the most complex work of an astronaut, performing artist, or composer, it is a passion for you to do it, do it well, and enjoy doing it. The disciplines it entails are not a choice for you but a necessity, like oxygen, food, and water.

Yet the passive-aggressive person is at best in a mood of apathy, saying, "I'd rather not," and at worst in a mood of inferiority, saying, "I'm afraid to attempt that." Career-guidance centers around the country assess the basic aptitudes of bright and capable people but often uncover these negative attitudes and the loss of confidence as impediments to the implementation of excellent aptitudes. As a result, personal therapy is often recommended in addition to career guidance.

No amount of therapy is enough, however, unless the person is also in a day-to-day skills-disciplining program that is under careful supervision. The learning goal is to develop confidence and continuity in a skill within the manifest capabilities of this person. The supervisor's aim is to "call out the gifts" of individuals and encourage them to believe in themselves by believing in them as their supervisor. There are all too few discussions of parent-child relationships in which it is noted that the absence of consistent, attentive supervision of the growing child in a skill that he or she enjoys and relishes is one of the roots of passive-aggressive life-styles.

If you are the counselor or teacher of such persons, it is not too late. You can focus upon the vocational heart of the person's being, develop a program of close supervision over a period of time, rebuild their confidence in the works of their hands, and help them develop the positive identity they need so badly.

As Christians, we usually speak of this process as the person's seriously searching out what God's calling is for his or her life and acting upon it in the immediate now. The glory of God shines about them and the beauty of the Lord rests upon them as God in Christ establishes the work of their hands (Ps. 90:16–17). This is the unique concern in the Christian care of these persons. While they are wandering aimlessly in the misty flats of their confusion of purpose and lack of direction in life, we as their fellow strugglers can lay a gentle but firm hand of encouragement on their shoulders while there is yet time—while it is day, as Jesus put it.

What were they put here by God to be and to do? We can ask the ancient question, *"Quo vadis?"* ("Where are you going?") We can stay with them as they find their own answers under God. All along the way we can say to them, *"Sursum corda!"* ("Lift up your hearts!") We are unto them a Barnabas, a person of encouragement, as we meet them in any "Interpreter's House" where we see people who do not know where they are going and fall into one crisis after another that drains them of hope, joy, and fulfillment under God.

6

The Mask
of Too Many Scruples

With the passive-aggressive person, perfectionism is a "hidden agenda." It is the flying colors and main publicity logo of the overscrupulous person. I use the word "overscrupulous" to describe this way of life because that word has such a long history in the religious communities of faith. DSM III uses the psychiatric term "compulsive personality disorder." Scrupulosity is a term used in Catholic moral theology for the behavior of people who overuse the confessional. They repeatedly confess trivial and minute sins. Not many Protestants have a formal confessional ritual. Nevertheless, all religious groups have overscrupulous communicants who frequently seek out a pastor for counseling, advice, and reassurance. They repeatedly express similar if not the same compulsive worries about trivial concerns. In churches of the revival tradition, they will use the invitation to make public profession of faith again and again. In many instances they have been baptized over and over. Other expressions of the overscrupulous way of life in the religious community will be discussed later in this chapter. These examples make clear the importance of including overscrupulosity in a discussion of religious behavior in personality disorders that psychiatrists describe as compulsive.

A Profile of the Overscrupulous Person in Action

Trivialization and Missing the Big Picture

Overscrupulous persons have great trouble seeing the woods for the trees. Their perfectionism about rules, efficiency, trivial details, or form interferes with their grasping the big picture. For example, they may have lost a list of things they are to remember. They will ransack the house, spend inordinate amounts of time looking for a particular list. The idea of relaxing, resting, and quietly re-creating the list from memory won't occur to them. No other list but the one they lost will do.

"Stinginess"

Overscrupulous persons are stingy in many ways. DSM III says that they are "stingy with their emotions and material possessions, for example, they rarely give compliments or gifts." They have a "restricted ability to express warm and tender emotions, e.g., the individual is unduly conventional, serious and formal" (pp. 326–327). Preoccupation with money, which is held in a Scrooge-like miserliness, is a hallmark of the overscrupulous person. Consequently, money becomes his or her battleground with family members, work associates, therapists, and others.

Controlling Others

Overscrupulous persons, being perfectionists, insist that other people do things their way. They are unaware of the rage that other people feel when their plans and pursuits are summarily set aside in behalf of such a person's often nit-picking demands. The overscrupulous go by the book. In a family or in the workplace, they function with a drill-instructor mentality.

Work Addiction

Being a confessed workaholic myself (See my *Confessions of a Workaholic*), I am uncomfortable writing this chapter. The reason, according to DSM III, is that "work and productivity are prized to the exclusion of pleasure and interpersonal relationships. When pleasure is considered, it is something to be planned and worked for. However, the individual keeps postponing the pleasurable activity, such as a vacation, so that it may never occur" (p. 326). It is important, however, to be realistic; this work-addiction pattern is a counterproductive way of doing one's work. I am grateful for the insight, perspective, and admonition of my two sons and my wife, who challenged me about the foolhardiness of the work addict's way of life. On the job itself, colleagues have taught me that it is best not to live as a slave on the job. Work addiction is not all that efficient, regardless of the compulsive worker's protestations as to how much, how well, and how long he or she has worked. Impatience with fellow workers and despair at the incompetency of persons in charge of the work situation so consume overscrupulous workers that their real productivity is highly constricted. Without the ability to live and let live, one finds that work is drudgery.

In a poll of 100 randomly selected physicians, A. Krakowski found that all declared themselves to be "compulsive personalities." Eighty percent possessed three of five criteria used for diagnosing compulsive personality disorder, and 20 percent satisfied four of the five criteria. These physicians had difficulty in relaxing, reluctance in taking vacations from work, problems in allocating time to their family, an inappropriate and excessive sense of responsibility for things beyond their control, chronic feelings of not doing enough, difficulty in setting limits, guilt feelings that interfered with the pursuit of pleasure, and the confusion of selfishness with healthy self-interest (Gabbard 1985).

One important observation to make about physicians, ministers, teachers, lawyers, air traffic controllers, and many others is that while they are performing specific and critical job procedures, it may be very important to strive for perfection. However, a surgeon who is off duty from the operating room, for example, need not be a perfectionist when teaching a son or daughter to ride a bike. In other words, if we can "corral" our perfectionism in the area of our specific skill performance, we can live the rest of life more serenely.

As in the case of passive-aggressive persons, scrupulous persons have trouble making decisions "because of an inordinate fear of making a mistake." Consequently they have a very hard time completing tasks. They ruminate about the minutiae to the neglect of the task as a whole.

Status Preoccupation

Scrupulous persons are hyperconscious of their status in a given organizational structure. They have endless wrangles and disappointments in the dominance-submission transactions in the workplace and in the home. One time they will be submissively obedient and the next time be all "dug in" in a pattern of stubborn defiance and insistence on being in charge. They are gifted—or cursed—with an intuitive capacity to play politics in the office or at home in order to see that their will is imposed on the rest of the crowd.

Religious Forms of Overscrupulous Behavior

In Handling the Church's Money

Churches do not always elect an overscrupulous person as treasurer, but often they do. I can recall visiting a church some distance away as a guest speaker. In order to get to the small city, I had to take an indirect flight. This flight cost forty-two dollars more than if I had gotten a direct flight to the city. I booked the flight costing forty-two dollars more. The treasurer did not ask me the cost of my ticket. He had already called the airlines and gotten the minimum fare! I was stuck with forty-two dollars excess travel expense. This story is a trivial one. But it illustrates how much more important to this man a trivial amount of money was than his personal relationship to me. I might add that upon handing me the check, he did not thank me for my services to the church. He seemed pained to have to let go of the check. I did not take this personally because I knew that for a compulsive personality the trivia block out people. Then, too, I had done him no injustice.

Another example of the overscrupulous, compulsive person is the church parliamentarian who keeps business meetings "in order." A long series of wrangling debates about points of order, procedures, and motions can exhaust this purely voluntary gathering. The tension is kept going by the nit-picking and fine-distinction-slicing of the person running the meeting and a few others of the same inclination. The wrangling may go on into the night until the only persons left are the church's full quorum of compulsive, overscrupulous people. All the rest have left the meeting because they have to work the next day.

"Tattling Among the Sinners"

Another example of the religious overscrupulous person is the person who feels it is his or her responsibility under God to report to the pastor every tiny infraction of the rules of the church, any behaviors inappropriate for members to be "caught" doing, and so on. "I just thought you ought to know what is going on, pastor," they will say. They are the self-appointed guardians of the rectitude of all the other members. If such a person is the teacher of a Sunday school class or the leader of a youth group, and the group is assigned to a particular room in the church property, the people being led and the place where they meet become the overscrupulous person's domain. "They are mine!" is the battle cry. As Millon says, "The compulsive's behavior conveys the attitude 'what is mine is mine and what is yours is yours; I will leave alone what is yours as long as you do likewise with mine'" (Millon 1981:229). They stake out their territory and guard its perimeter fiercely.

Biblical Nit-Picking

Probably the most pandemic expression of overscrupulous religiosity is seen in some people's interpretation of certain sections of the Bible. *Which* verses from the Bible they center upon varies from person to person. The disordered personality chooses passages that are tailor-made to his or her private biases. Yet these particular passages of scripture are test cases, "litmus tests" for the acceptability of the overscrupulous person's worth as a Christian. All other testimony of the whole Bible and the whole counsel of God is irrelevant. In these texts the compulsive, overscrupulous person stakes out his or her territory in the Bible. You either stay within that territory with the person or you are an unbeliever, an outsider, a stranger to the commonwealth of the people of God as far as he or she is concerned.

The Scrupulosity of the Religiously "Damned"

More poignant than those instances I have mentioned, however, is the thought life of some overscrupulous people when they are going through major stresses. A parent may have died, or both parents in too rapid succession. A job is lost because the company has gone bankrupt, been sold to new owners, or joined a megaconglomerate. This person, by whose methodical, repetitive actions people could set their watches during the day, is now out of work. A long-suffering spouse has had it, and is abandoning the marriage, or has found a good job just as the compulsive partner faces retirement.

In such crises, compulsive religious persons begin to be obsessive about religion. At first they are filled with a generalized anxiety. Then a specific scripture passage, such as Hebrews 6:4–6ff., takes hold of their thoughts and tells them that they are lost and beyond God's reach because they have crucified Christ afresh as an apostate. Or they feel that they have sinned against the Holy Spirit and therefore cannot be forgiven. They become agitated and depressed and refuse to be reassured or comforted. In these instances, they are beyond rational persuasion. They need the help of a psychiatrist who works in conjunction with a pastor who is skilled in counseling. Such persons are probably clinically depressed and may have suicidal thoughts. Their depressions usually have agitated and apprehensive features. The binds in which events trap them terrorize them with fears of embarrassment and ridicule.

Sources of Empathy for the Overscrupulous

We get the picture of persons who live stingily, orderly, and obstinately. How can we enter into the world of these persons and develop some understanding of how they came to be this way? How can we learn more about their suffering so that the quality of our mercy will not be strained? In the life of the church and the practice of the Christian faith, such people hold the church together with their insistence upon "order," and at the same time they create enough resentment to blow it apart. They are legalists with a vengeance. But again, they create the same "toe-the-line" responses in us. In their legalistic push for the justice in the minutiae of the law, and in our fighting responses to them, though, as Shakespeare says, "in the course of justice none of us should see salvation." Therefore, we "pray for mercy,/ And that same prayer doth teach us all to render/ The deeds of mercy" (*The Merchant of Venice* IV, i, 184).

An "Unnecessary Conscience"

The anxiety of scrupulous persons clusters around the need to be in control of themselves and others. They were trained by parents and by teachers to "behave," to stay in line, and their most minute behavior was supervised. This was not accompanied by the warm cuddliness in which the dependent person swam. The parent in this instance is punitive for actions seen as infractions of control, and restraints are enforced with anger, threats, and exclusion. By the time the child gets to school, he or she is perceived by teachers as the "good" child. Conformity is fueled by the fear of intimidation. I met such a child's father after a church service in a Southern community. He was a farmer. He himself was warm and caring toward his seven-year-old daughter. I do not know what kind of care the mother gave. However, he was worried about his child. I asked him what was wrong and he said, "She has an *unnecessary* conscience." She was afraid to go back to school. At school she had been asked to go to the blackboard and write something. She did it well. Inadvertently, however, she put the chalk in her pocket and forgot about it until she got home. When she found it she was terrified at what a great wrong she had done. She was afraid to go back to school for fear the teacher would punish her for stealing. He said, "Don't you think that is an unnecessary conscience?" I heartily agreed with him and introduced him to a family service agency, suggesting that he and the mother go there with the child. Of course, I asked that they themselves be very gentle with her and calm her fears of themselves and the teacher.

Religion as a Conductor of Parental Overcontrol

Religious teachings easily become the medium of parental overcontrol, taking many directions. Children are taught that if they do not do as they are told, Jesus will not love them. They are not then told, after they have been obedient, that Jesus *is* loving them for it and is proud of them. At least that would be half a loaf of mercy. They get little or no positive appreciation for doing the things they are supposed to do. They are not thanked for spontaneous goodness. The theological mayhem of placing conditions on Jesus' love pushes this growing child into thinking of God as an enemy who "will get you if you don't watch out." God becomes a "stingy" God.

Religious Ritual and Parental Overcontrol

Both organized religion and growing children have a passion for ritual. A little child, when filled with glee by a simple game of catching something he or she drops, wants to "do it again." A boy may like to sit in the same place in the same room as his grandmother peels an apple for him. Or a girl may want only her older sister to comb and arrange her hair. More than this, the day is given its structure for a child by rituals of awakening, being cleansed, fed, and kept clean, being led into activities, enabled and encouraged to rest. In the process a relationship is built between child and parents. As Erik Erikson (1977:78) says, ritual is "a deepening communality, a proven ceremonial form, and a timeless quality from which all participants emerge with a sense of awe and purification." The sadness of the overscrupulous person is that when the ritual loses its communal quality it becomes a lonely, isolated experience that means something punishing to them while to others it brings peace and joy.

Some rituals of religion, such as confession, pastoral counseling, making a profession of faith in a revival, being baptized, and attending all of the church services, are latched onto by compulsive, overscrupulous persons, as I have indicated before in this chapter. They become addicted to these rituals. They seem laden with guilt and suffer continual temptation. They anxiously do everything that is expected of them and that they are supposed to do, scrupulously out of fear of divine punishment. In addition to this, they walk among the rest of the membership of the congregation, keeping tabs on them. They often confront other people under inappropriate circumstances: "Why weren't you at Sunday school? Aren't you going to stay for church? I never see you at prayer meeting."

The poignant aspect of this scrupulosity and their harassment of other people is that such persons become more and more isolated. The creative function of religious ritual is to bring people into open, teachable, and forgiving community with each other. In the extreme conformity of overscrupulous persons just the opposite occurs. They become isolated as other people avoid them. Another painful aspect of this loneliness is their grimness and humorlessness.

Biblical Wisdom and Understanding of the Overscrupulous

Jesus' teachings are filled with his resistance to the official religious teachers, who systematically demanded an unbearable load of scrupulosity of their followers. He was concerned for the individual victims. He was seeking to change the system that reinforced and demanded this burdensome legalism. Compare the compulsive conformist's preoccupation with trivia to the neglect of the big picture with Matthew 23:23–24: "You tithe mint and dill and cummin, and have neglected the weightier matters of the law, justice and mercy and faith; these you ought to have done, without neglecting the others. You blind guides, straining out a gnat and swallowing a camel!"

Jesus looked upon the people as being like sheep without a shepherd, harassed and helpless under the intolerable load of such quibbling religion in its disregard for the largeness of the loving heart of God. He spoke to them about the crushing load of overscrupulous religion, particularly when it became the only diet provided for spiritually famished people. He said, "Come to me, all who labor and are heavy laden, and I will give you rest. Take my yoke upon you, and learn of me; for I am gentle and lowly in heart, and you will find rest for your souls. For my yoke is easy, and my burden is light" (Matt. 11:28–30).

The apostle Paul saw the day come when followers of this gentle Jesus would fall back into the hard legalisms from which they had been delivered through the grace of God in Christ. He chided them for reintroducing the blind compulsiveness of the scrupulously followed rituals as a flight from the life for which Christ had set them free. He said to them, "Formerly, when you did not know God, you were in bondage to beings that by nature are no gods; but now that you have come to know God, or rather to be known by God, how can you turn back again to the weak and beggarly elemental spirits, whose slaves you want to be once more? You observe days, and months, and seasons, and years!" (Gal. 4:8–10).

They had reverted to the mindless ritualism that in itself was a harsh caricature of whatever living faith it had originally sought to celebrate. The tyranny of these rituals in "corporation religion" puts money in the treasuries of the slick operators of the system. One such system prompted Martin Luther, on October 31, 1517, to nail his "Ninety-five Theses" on the castle church door in Wittenberg, Germany. They were aimed at the money indulgences collected at the confessional booths. Private penance, administered by the clergy, exacted money of the penitent. Thus people "bought" their forgiveness and merit from God. As Luther said, "They preach only human doctrines who say that as soon as the money clinks into the money chest, the soul flies out of purgatory. It is certain that when money clinks in the money chest, greed and avarice can be increased; but when the church intercedes the result is in the hands of God alone." No religious group can smugly say that this greed and avarice is a sixteenth-century problem. Similar capers appear in churches and on television religious "shows" daily. Compulsive, overscrupulous people pay for their gullibility.

Yet Isaiah's contradiction is the healing grace that the burdened, driven, unloved, and often unlovable overscrupulous person needs to feel: "Ho, every one who thirsts, come to the waters; and he who has no money, come, buy and eat! Come, buy wine and milk without money and without price" (Isa. 55:1).

God is not a God who always stands over against these persons who feel that they have to work their fingers to the bone simply to survive in God's presence. God in Jesus Christ is the one who comes alongside them. They are not required to be perfect, or to hoard up merit and security through the things they produce. God is a lifter of burdens that by the nature of our human limitations inevitably must be borne. More than that, God removes unnecessary burdens of resentment, guilt, and nameless fears. God planted in us an affinity and an aptitude for loving God and one another unconditionally and being loved by God and others with grace. This is not a cheap grace or one that takes wrongdoing lightly. The very heart of grace is forgiveness of mistakes, temptations, and sins. Overscrupulous persons need this kind of message acted out in relation to their lives. God has acted in Jesus Christ, and enables us to be "kind to one another, tenderhearted, forgiving one another," as God in Christ forgave us (Eph. 4:31).

Living, Working with, and Caring for the Overscrupulous Person

Overscrupulous persons have been overcontrolled in the earliest patterning of their life. If they are in the driver's seat, their right foot hovers just above the brake at all times. If you are in the driver's seat and they are your passenger, their fists are tight; they sit on the edge of the seat and supervise your driving. This can be a nerve-racking trip!

How is one to live and work with and care for such people? We must bear in mind that they are more disposed to suffer in their bondage than to cast off their bonds and enter the freedom of a life of spontaneity and grace. They have become accustomed to their bonds. Several quite concrete suggestions are valuable.

Listen to Their Muscles and Breathing

These persons are filled with inner tensions. It transparently shows in the muscles of their hands and face, the way they sit, the way they pace back and forth, and how they labor for breath. Breath does not have to be "labored" for, in persons who have no physical obstructions in their breathing equipment. It is free! These signs of tension are nonverbal messages to which the person of patience listens compassionately, with eyes as well as ears. The beginning of a ministry of encouragement to these driven persons is slowly, deliberately, and warmly to slow them down. Remember: you may appear as another taskmaster or competitor to these people. Do not accept either part in the drama of their lives. You are the one who decides on a part; they are not the ones who automatically assign you a role. Choose the part of a character they have not included in their script, one that is a stranger to them: *Be an encouraging spirit.* If they insist upon perceiving you as a drill instructor demanding conformity and precision, you can issue one order that the compulsive person tends not to hear: "At ease!" Every really competent drill instructor has an underside of humor, gentleness, and encouragement beneath his or her demand for obedience.

Stress Interpretation, Reduction, and Management

As persons of encouragement, you and I can enter into the world of the compulsive and overscrupulous with genuine warmth and empathy by becoming fellow stressed persons with them. Specific recurrent stress situations can be reviewed in detail, and procedures for understanding, reducing, and managing the stress can be taught them. As given as they are to "rules" of behavior, they tend to substitute your creative, adaptive rules for some of their more destructive, exhausting rituals. Overscrupulous persons fall into the category of the Type A personality. Many times driven persons come to your attention and are open for dialogue in relation to sheer exhaustion or some physical ailment that unremitting stress and their churning emotions have conspired to generate. This becomes a teachable moment for coaching them supportively as to how they can manage stress and enjoy life more. (Several manuals are helpful in this process; see Friedman and Rosenman 1974, Oates 1985, and Selye 1976.)

This approach does not cast them in the "sick" role, although the wear and tear of stress does record itself in the health of the body. Rather, it enables you and me to present ourselves as fellow burden bearers and encourage them to join the many others for whom life had become a taskmaster but who now find it a source of joy merely tempered by responsibility.

Creative Interruptions of Incessant Demands

The incessant demands that overscrupulous persons place upon themselves, their fellow workers, and their families fasten a viselike grip on their whole system of relationships. It is not only their bodies that show the wear and tear; their marriages do also. As one such person said to me, "Work starts off being something you do. It then becomes something you are. And at last it becomes *all* that you are." If, as we believe as Christians, marriage is a process in which two people become one flesh, it is inevitable that the marital partner of the overscrupulous person will begin to suffer. This may be your or my point of entry into that person's confidence. The threat of abandonment, separation, divorce, or "acting out" behavior in a spouse or a child has a way of getting the attention of compulsive, overscrupulous persons when hopes for insight on their part fail. A family crisis ensues. You as a pastor, a relative, a friend, or a co-worker become a confidant.

One intervention you can propose is that they take time out from their regular routine. This time-out can be a forty-eight-hour trip to a nearby state park or an economy weekend package at a hotel in a nearby city. This interruption has a way of breaking the grip that routine has upon their way of life. If the family likes to camp, this can be done even more economically. Such an intervention challenges the stinginess of the overscrupulous, penny-pinching person. It is a different kind of investment, an investment in relationships, not commodities that can be hoarded. Investments in relationships do not corrode, moths cannot eat them, nor can thieves break through and steal.

If this prescription for the family is beneficial, then this could become a ritual to replace some of the forced marches of work that the compulsive father or mother uses the weekends and other free times to accomplish. Suggest that they try it; they might like it!

Interruptions may be of less expense, less duration in time, and happen on a daily basis. A relaxation ritual can both fit into and relieve the strain of the person's orderliness. The day can be interrupted, for example, with the simple process of the relaxation response described by Herbert Benson (1975: 27). He suggests that twice daily a person take twenty minutes and do four things:

1. Find a quiet environment at work or at home where you can be uninterrupted.
2. Choose a "mental device" such as a favorite word, a favorite color, a favorite peaceful scene, or a relaxing memory and focus your attention upon it, repeating it over and over in your mind.
3. Take a passive, receiving attitude that enables you to "receive" from the air you breathe and the world of which you are a part, as over against an active, pushing, aggressive, taking, earning attitude.

4. Maintain a comfortable physical position, removing all pressure, strain, and demand on your body.

If the person practicing the relaxation response is a religious person, this whole experience may be one of prayer. However, the prayer attitude would be one of thinking of God as sustainer, encourager, renewer, healer, and friend. Thoughts of God as taskmaster and punisher are *verboten,* forbidden. Jesus' invitation "Come unto me, all you who labor . . . , and I will give you rest" is a good choice for a thought to fix in one's mind.

Thinking About God

The core concern you and I can address with overscrupulous persons is, "What is *your* God like?" These persons tend to have a Pharaoh for their god. This god is one of perpetual demand who expects them to "make bricks without straw," for whom their labor is their only access to him (or her). This god never says, "You are my son or daughter in whom I am well pleased." If they are Christians, Jesus is the one who expects them to scour land and sea making converts for him. If they do not do so every hour on the hour, their own souls are in danger of hellfire because they failed to witness for him. He is the one who stands unforgivingly at the slightest infraction. They are to go to confession repeatedly or are to ask for salvation over and over again.

The whole perception of a God of deliverance from the slave pits of making bricks without straw, a God of participation with them as a co-laborer in creation, a God of redemption and release from the burden of guilt, shame, and sin, a God who has a "wideness in his mercy" and whose love is broader than the measure of a person's mind—this is the perception you and I want to convey by our presence and our responses to these burden bearers who take on the world's loads.

Conveying this kind of relationship to God is best done over a continuing pilgrimage of spiritual direction. Longer-term therapeutic relationships, if indeed the person chooses such a course, are most sustaining and productive in their lives. Dramatic and sudden changes rarely take place, and "quick evangelism" fits into their compulsive rituals all too easily. Hence, more patient spiritual guidance and day-by-day and week-by-week attentiveness speak to their condition both in individual counseling and in small-group relationships.

7

The Mask
of Detachment from Life

Some people live a way of life *detached* from other people, but not all are detached in the same way.

Some are detached in a passive way. They are too emotionally and socially deprived to dare to think they could be of any special importance to other people. As Harry Stack Sullivan (1947:41) says, they "have not grasped the possibility that they may be valued, cherished by others." In prayer, I think, these persons are like the publican in Jesus' parable. They will not even lift their eyes up to heaven, since they assume that they are not cherished by God either. To use the Quaker understanding of "concerns," they present themselves as *unconcerned.*

Other detached people are actively detached. They purposely avoid forming lasting attachments to other people. They have to be given strong or even absolute assurances that they will be accepted uncritically on their own terms beforehand. They are easily humiliated and hypersensitive to rejection. As a result they are detached from most people. They are "one-way covenant" people—that is, their relationship to others is on *their* terms. As DSM III says, "They may have one or two close friends, but these are contingent and unconditional" (p. 323).

DSM III identifies the first type of detached persons as "schizoid" or "asocial" personalities. The second group are "avoidant" personalities. In this discussion, I am choosing to hold them in relation to each other in one chapter, so we can keep the central feature of detachment in the forefront of our attention. They differ uniquely, though, in that schizoid personalities are socially isolated and evince little desire for social relations, but avoidant personalities yearn for acceptance and approval. Avoidant persons exact such unlimited loyalty from others, however, that few people want to get involved with them. As contrasted with passive-detaching individuals, they are not unconcerned but super-concerned. The end result of detachment is the same. Let us consider first the passive, asocial, or schizoid personality and then the actively detached, avoidant personality disorder.

The Passively Detached Person

Do not think that passively detached persons are eccentric in their speech, mannerisms, or thought patterns. They are not. They are more likely to be seen in every walk of life.

> They appear untroubled and indifferent, and function adequately in their occupations, but they are judged by their associates as rather colorless and shy, seeming to prefer to be by themselves and lacking in the need to communicate or relate affectionately to others. Typically they remain in the background of social life, work quietly and unobtrusively at their jobs, and are rarely noticed by those with whom they have routine contact. They would fade into the passing scene to live their lives in a tangential undisturbed inconspicuousness were it not for the fact there are persons who expect or wish them to be more vibrant, alive and involved. (Millon 1981:273)

This thumbnail sketch may bring up on the screen of your memory many schoolmates, fellow work associates, and relatives. However, if you happen to be married to someone with this detached way of life, you may live a life of frustration because you expect warmth, affection, and demonstrativeness. It is not there. You might think that the person *intentionally* does not love you, care for you, or have any feeling at all for you. However, this is not necessarily so. He or she is intrinsically bland, colorless, and imperceptive of your needs.

Poverty of feelings and thought is the most important feature of the passively detached, asocial person. We live in a glad-hand culture that highly values outgoing persons. This is especially true in the life of the churches. Churches want pastors who meet people easily, who take a lot of initiative toward others, and who are warm and vibrant. When they get such a pastor, that pastor in turn puts pressure on each member of the congregation to be outgoing, to make visitors warmly welcome, and to shake hands and greet the next person in the pew. They may even want people to hug the person next to them!

In an atmosphere like this, passively detached and asocial

personalities are not alarmed, upset, or hostile about such demands. If they comply, they simply go through the motions mechanically and without feeling. The flatness of their emotionality befuddles the dyed-in-the-wool glad-handers. Yet detached duties, such as preparing the envelopes for a mailing from the church, may be the kind of task that they will do well. Such a job would drive a pushy, glad-handing, outgoing person up the wall.

Vocationally, the withdrawn, detached person may perform work in isolation quite well. The forester who spends a great deal of time alone can be this asocial and still function quite well. I have noticed, for example, that whereas some librarians are highly social beings, others are asocial persons who do the appointed tasks well but live solitary, isolated existences. This is not to say that they make *better* librarians, just that the work itself appeals to withdrawn, asocial people.

Teachers and professors who teach asocial people and are responsible for grooming them for remunerative employment are hard pressed to place them in a kind of work that permits them to be as detached as they are. Similarly, in professional and graduate schools I have noticed that a significant number of such detached persons gravitate toward detached kinds of work—experimental lab work, abstract translating, radiology, pathology. Yet when they are pulled out of their absorption in the world of objects and into social interaction with others they are inarticulate, painfully shy, and at best wallflowers.

In one of his earlier books, Seward Hiltner presented a vignette of such a shy person. She was a nineteen-year-old woman who had finished high school a year before and was interested in art. The pastors of her church had become aware of her needs from other members of a group in the church she attended. They said they were having difficulty enabling her to feel at home in the group.

When one of the pastors conversed with her, her own report was that she did not have much in common with the other members of the group because she was older. They had jobs and she had not been able to find one in her chosen field of art. Her estimate of herself was: "Oh, I don't know, I'm not very good at anything. I like to draw and paint, but I know I could never make a go of it . . . there's so much competition—well, I've just stopped thinking about it." She continued to say that she would rather not engage in dancing with a group, would rather not join in singing with them. The pastor says that he "missed the boat in trying to urge her into social activities." Hiltner (1952:49–50) suggests that with these shy people "we can express genuine interest and understanding without becoming overcome by any vested interest in keeping group activity going. And we can be patient, knowing that, having done this, we need to await the action of the Holy Spirit, making the person ready to seek help if he [or she] needs it."

Yet one of the most taxing aspects of withdrawn, asocial persons is that they do not *interest* other people. To the contrary, they tend to bore them. When you seek to establish a personal friendship, a church relationship, or an individual personal counseling relationship, they do not take up with you where you left off in your last meeting with them. You must start all over again to develop some degree of warmth. After several such starts many people give up trying. This confirms asocial persons in their automatic assumption that they are of no account, and that it is only natural for people to fail to see anything desirable in them. In turn, they continue as they are—avoiding at one and the same time both the effort and the punishment involved in interpersonal relationships.

Therefore, in caring for withdrawn, asocial persons, you are caught in the dilemma between your own imperative to be interested in, have warm feelings for, and enjoy these persons, on the one hand, and the fact that they bore you, show no warmth for you, and seem not to enjoy the pleasure of your company.

This dilemma initiates a cruel circularity. The person is not interested in anything you mention. The "cat dies" at the end of each of your attempts to interest this person, as he or she responds merely with a "Well," "Oh," "Is that so?," or "Yes," "No." Then you lose interest as you give up trying. Erich Fromm (1973:273) pinpoints the human issue in this struggle:

> If somebody says, "I am bored," he usually means to say something about the world outside, indicating that it does not provide him with interesting or amusing stimuli. But when we speak of a "boring person" we refer to the person himself, to his character. We do not mean that he is boring today because he has not told us an interesting story; when we say he is a boring person we mean that he is boring *as a person.* There is something dead, unalive, uninteresting in him.

Rarely do we address the profound spiritual condition of *being* a bore. Søren Kierkegaard (1944:238) says, "Boredom is the root of all evil, and it is this that must be kept at distance. Boredom is aptly an inborn genial aptitude, partly an acquired immediacy." He likens it to tedium and speaks autobiographically:

> How terrible tedium is—terribly tedious; I know no stronger expression, for only the like is known by the like. If only there were some higher, stronger expression, then there would be at least a movement. I lie stretched out, inactive; the only thing I see is emptiness. The only thing I move about in is emptiness. I do not even suffer pain. (Kierkegaard 1944:29)

It seems to me that the opposite of boredom is curiosity. In understanding and responding to the spiritual situation of the apathetic, asocial person, can the warmth of response and sparking interest of curiosity come into his or her being?

The Spiritual Situation and Renewal of the Passively Detached Person

Focusing on the Sense of Worthlessness

The most significant spiritual issue in the profile of passively detached persons is their sense of worthlessness, their persistent discounting of themselves. They seem to have a native inability to express themselves verbally, affectionately, or with vigor. The world responds to them as if this makes them worthless, of no account, to be pushed aside by a touching, feeling, and aggressive world. It does not take much time in conversation for this personal self-estimate of theirs to emerge. In the vignette of a case presented by Seward Hiltner, the woman says: "I'm not much good. . . . I'm not very good at anything. . . . I wouldn't get anywhere. . . . It's really no use." Instead of trying to push her into more social activity, Hiltner held that it is a better approach to focus on this sense of worthlessness, to challenge it, and to refuse to agree with it. This need not be done aggressively; you can simply call attention to the person's self-estimate and *wonder* where it all got started. This wondering can help your boredom. It may even be the beginning of the person's curiosity. A mutual wondering about the automatic thoughts that spring out of his or her conversation is a top priority item for a continuing agenda.

Admittedly, such a person may have had a native unresponsiveness from birth, and as a result the parents may have given little cuddling and affection. The "average" child with full neurological equipment at birth may turn out the same way. He or she may have been brought up by stoical parents who were stingy with warmth, impersonal and cold. This does not make these persons worthless, even though they themselves may draw that conclusion. They matter. When you or I challenge this as contradictory to the image of God in which they are made, this may be the beginning of a glimmer of surprise in them. As Jesus said, they may not think they have the value of a sparrow, but they are not forgotten by God and are valued far above sparrows. They are not to be afraid. They are of great worth. They are made in God's image, and they have been bought with the price of the life of Christ.

Attending to Their Nonverbal Messages

The poverty of the verbal response of passively detached persons may distract attention from their nonverbal messages. For example, these people do get married. Usually they marry a person who is aggressive and talkative and who takes practically all the initiative in courtship and planning for marriage. After settling into a daily routine after marriage, the more aggressive mate sets about to "change" the passively detached partner. Frustration results. In marriage and family therapy, the aggressive partner is the one who seeks help. One of the complaints is that the spouse does not demonstrate love and affection. Passively detached partners do not *say* they love their mate, nor do they usually initiate sexual relations.

Aggressive partners can be encouraged to observe the nonverbal ways such a mate lets them know things. The nonverbal husband may repair a household appliance, meet his wife at work on a rainy day in the car so she does not have to ride the bus, or stay with the children so she can have some free time. She married a very shy person, and shy people talk this way!

In pastoral counseling, social isolates may write down what they have to say and hand it to the counselor at the beginning of an interview. Or they may make something for the counselor, such as a needlework creation, a kind of art, or some kind of food. These nonverbal messages say what they think. I have found that these persons occasionally turn out to be inveterate letter writers.

These ways of nonverbal communication are what the whole field of expressive therapy is about. Its media include art, writing, pantomime, dance, music, and pet therapy. It uses all possible ways of attending to the nonverbal messages of withdrawn persons to establish a continuing relationship.

The Consecration of the Solitary Life

The social isolation of the withdrawn, asocial person says something about what is missing in our exceptionally gregarious formation of the Christian community. Even a hermit in the desert prays with a distant church in mind. Yet this appreciation of solitariness is difficult to find in the life of the churches.

The monastic life of the Catholic, Eastern Orthodox, and to some extent the Anglican churches provides a carefully defined and historically tested structure for persons to live lives of praise to God through the disciplines of chastity, poverty, and obedience. Some orders, such as the Trappists, build their community life around a core of silence. Similarly, the Quaker fellowship sanctions silence and the complines of nonverbal but not verbal communion. The unprogrammed meeting removes talkativeness from the center of the life of worship of God. It might be added that there is also a consecration of the works of the hands in manual labor.

God must be trying to tell us something significant about the importance of manual intelligence alongside verbal intelligence in such tests as the Wechsler Adult Intelligence scale. Nonverbal intelligence uses a major part of the world's creative production. It seems to me that the pastoral counselor and the Christian community have a special way of affirming the solitariness of the asocial person, a way not available in the heavily competitive world of business, commerce, and all those aspects of our society that put a high premium on folksy chat. Jesus himself, when he wanted to pray, not only went into the synagogue, as his custom was. It is also recorded that in the morning, "a great while before day, he rose and went out to a lonely place, and there he prayed" (Mark 1:35). The psalmist declares, "Father of the fatherless and protector of widows is God in his holy habitation. God gives the desolate a home to dwell in" (Ps. 68:5–6). Jesus said, "I will not leave you desolate; I will come to you" (John 14:18). Whereas asocial persons have too much distance and lack deep feeling about other people, you and I can learn something of great value from them—the value of more distance from the overstimulation of the myriad associates, groups, and crowds in which we daily immerse ourselves. In learning to appreciate socially detached persons, we just may express that grace of

which they have long been deprived—making them aware
that they are valued and loved just as they are. We may make
connection with that warmth deep in the center of their being.
Once we have done so, we may find in them trusted and
valued friends for the rest of our lives.

The Actively Detached Person

Only recently have psychiatric diagnosticians separated out
actively detached persons from passively detached persons.
As they have done so, they have noted the marked difference
in the pattern of child-rearing in these two kinds of lonely,
isolated people.

Passively detached people usually have a history of *withheld*
warmth, affection, and mental stimulation. To the contrary,
the actively detached not only experienced such withholding,
they received in addition outright rejection, ridicule, depreci-
ation, denigration, belittlement, and humiliation. The most
common catch-all term for this today is "verbal abuse." As a
result, emotional and intellectual disability has been built into
their life. They have learned to expect such treatment from
everyone. They stay out of the way of possible rejection and
humiliation. Theodore Millon gave them their diagnostic
name—*avoidant* personalities.

It may well be that these persons are the most seriously
impaired individuals we have yet discussed. They are most
prone to anxiety disorders, phobic disorders, obsessive-com-
pulsive disorders, bodily illnesses, chronic depression, and
schizophrenic disorders when their repertoire of avoidant
coping devices collapses. Therefore we need all the help we
can get from professionally trained persons in seeing to it that
these severely damaged individuals are patiently restored to
their rightful inheritance as human beings bearing the image
of the Creator. If we see verbal abuse, ridicule, and humiliation of little children going on in our direct observation of
families, we need enough courage to enter into the family
system and suggest that the parents talk with their pediatri-
cian or with a family and children's agency about the child's
tension and insecurity. If in school the child shows marked
loss of feelings of competence and confidence, then parents
can be encouraged by teachers to go to a child evaluation
center related to a university department of pediatrics. In
groups of adolescents, if we detect that a particular youth is
the continual object of ridicule, we can intervene with our
own person. We can demand that the whole group pause and

discuss what this is all about. Why pick on this one person? Why not pass some of this negative attention around to others, if it has to be? Then again, does it have to be? Personal attention to those being hazed, given with a genuine desire to enhance their self-worth, can begin building a sense of genuine appreciation and trust.

The Assumptive World of the Actively Detached Adult

Once a person has reached early adulthood, the active detachment patterns of behavior are full-blown. These behaviors are based upon the assumption that *all* people they meet will continue forever to reject, humiliate, ridicule, and disparage them just as those responsible for their rearing did. They move on the assumption that their parents' and possibly their siblings' assessment of them is true. Therefore they assume that they are not worthy of esteem from themselves and others. Any achievement of theirs is "nothing." Their personal shortcomings fill them with dismay. They assume that the world is a harsh place; they have therefore concluded long ago that life is hard to bear. They meet life with mixed emotions of sadness, anger, loneliness, and a feeling of alienation from other people.

The Actively Detached Person's Resulting Behaviors

With such a worldview, avoidant personalities respond by excessive social withdrawal. They are extremely reluctant to form personal attachments for fear of being hurt. Their "distance machinery" works overtime. They are reluctant to get involved in social or vocational commitments. They live their lives on the periphery of the action in their social and vocational spheres. For example, if you are eager to involve them in the activities of the church, they exaggerate their unworthiness and beg off from making any promises to attend, participate, or lead.

Furthermore, they are supersensitive to rejection and slights and stay intensely alert for the slightest sign of social embarrassment, downgrading, or humiliation. The most innocent, guileless comment or action of others they interpret as a personal insult. A light touch of humor can become a federal case of ridicule to them.

As they warily and cagily venture into any kind of personal relationship to an individual or group, they protect themselves unduly. They demand elaborate reassurances and guarantees from the other person. Yet they expect to be accepted uncritically and without conditions. Any hint of a negative response is devastating and catastrophic. They are hypervigilant, watching and waiting for rejection.

The end result of these assumptions and behaviors is to create the very thing they fear. As Shakespeare said of guilt, avoidance "spills itself in fearing to be split." Avoidants, as Proverbs 28:1 avers, "flee when no one pursues." People *do* lose patience with them, are turned off by them, and have as little to do with them as possible. Few people stop, look, and listen when such exaggerated response comes their way. Life is too short—they are likely to say—for them to put up with this. Or they have enough problems of their own and do not want to take on this person's mixed messages of both affection and mistrust.

However, if you are different and can overlook the overreactions of avoidant persons, you may be intrigued by the deeper, more poignant dimensions of their being. You can rightly assume that you are not the only person to whom they react as they have to you. They confuse other people, too, with the distortions that their mistrust creates. If you slow down and hear their apartness, their alienation, their essential loneliness, you may overhear the inner voices of their past speaking to them: "You are no good. You are stupid and useless. I wish you had never been born. I wish I had never seen you." Verbal abuse—twenty years, thirty years later! Today they are thin-skinned, heavily guarding themselves against real and imagined emotional pain as the primary value of their lives. They cut themselves off from other people and hide under a protective coloration of unimportance, insignificance, and inconspicuousness. Thus, they erect defenses against a world they perceive to be violent. You can readily appreciate, then, how vulnerable they are. How can one relate effectively to them?

Spiritual Concerns and Care of the Actively Detached

Knee-Jerk Responses to Injustice

As you and I project ourselves into the situation of a small child, a young boy or girl, or an adolescent being tongue-lashed unmercifully and unremittingly by an adult, we feel a keen sense of injustice on their behalf. I have heard parents do this in public places such as restaurants. I have called it off in family counseling sessions. I have been caught between the two, in the cross fire of humiliating exposure of children and young people in churches of which I have been pastor. We are committed to the expectation of the Lord, as voiced by Micah, that we do justly, love mercy, and walk humbly with God. It seems to me that the intention of God in relation to children is to turn, transform, or convert the hearts of parents to a just, merciful, and humble treatment of children.

When, therefore, I sense that persons are actively detaching themselves from the significant people in their lives, the first deeply religious concern I think is being expressed is a knee-jerk reflex of injustice that has its origins in the earliest formation of their worldview. Their sense of injustice is so sharply edged that the slightest tap puts it into uncontrolled action. The distance they create is so necessary to them that backing off, taking a calmer, more patient pace in building a relationship an inch at a time rather than in long strides, is the better part of wisdom and the greater part of considerateness. It is to act "according to knowledge," as the apostle Paul says.

Before the whole issue of the inbred hypersensitivity to injustice is made a part of the agenda for spiritual direction, the *mistrust* of actively detached persons must be gradually thawed. These persons have given up hope that they will be able to see the goodness of God in the land of living human beings. As Erik Erikson (1964:118) says, "Hope is the enduring belief in the attainability of fervent wishes, in spite of the dark urges and rages that mark the beginning of existence." At the beginnings of their existence, avoidant individuals were saturated with injustices, causing them to lose hope that *any* human relationship would be just, merciful, and humble.

Consequently, to be a source of slowly growing hope for these very demanding human beings is the beginning of trust. To do this, clear covenants carefully kept and open to being tested and tried are necessary. As each attempt to break off dealings with you and me occurs, we can sustain our relationship by seeing it as a test, not as a personal rejection. My usual statement in making promises to people in general, but especially with an avoidant person, is that I will promise little and do more rather than promise more and do less.

As your and my spiritual direction becomes trustworthy with increasing signs of hope, the main concern of the history of injustice they have suffered, especially in their formative years, emerges somewhat naturally. To reframe the "dark urges and rage" they experience as *feelings of injustice* may well create what David Augsburger calls "interpathy," as contrasted with empathy. Empathy is that process in which you imaginatively put yourself in the place of the other person. Interpathy recognizes that you cannot do this, but you are eager to learn from the other person what his or her being is like. If you and I have not come from a heritage of personal humiliation, derogation, and ridicule, we are a little phony when we say that we "know" what it is like. Yet we share a common passion for justice and want them to teach us about the injustices they have suffered. If we have not been premature, there is hope that a genuine alliance can thus be formed and sustained. If we too quickly convey that we "know" just how they feel, they can more quickly tell us, "Nobody knows the trouble I've seen."

Promises and Disappointments

As I have said, to promise little and do more is exceptionally important in relating to actively detaching persons. Equally so, exacting promises of them is hazardous. In this respect, the church's demands that people make long-term commitments fall on deaf ears. We can learn much from the ways in which alcoholics make extravagant promises of sobriety and quickly break them, thereby severing the relationship in their flood of remorse. Conversely, the actively detaching person will not make any commitment unless you and I make large—and unrealistic—promises to them. In both cases, not to corner them into promises is a considerate way to care for them. To be very careful not to promise too much is likewise important. An invitation with no strings attached is enough and to spare, yet this runs counter to party-line religious interpretations of total commitment on the spot. Jesus' wisdom of invitation, of standing at the door and knocking, of awaiting an invitation, of living in the day that is at hand with no thought of the tomorrows, certainly speaks to the actively detaching person's condition more than do our more pressured tactics.

The actively avoidant human being entered adult life with "wounds that draw no blood." The injuries of verbal abuse to children today are obscured by the media emphasis upon sexual abuse, which in itself is an evil kept in force by verbal abuse. However, both within and without the church, family verbal abuse can take all sorts of religious garb.

Verbal abuse in religious families and groups may come very early when parents condemn a young child with threats of God's rejection. "Jesus is ashamed of you for not remembering your Bible verses in church today. Aren't you ashamed

of yourself?" "You cried when we left you in the nursery
today. You made us miss church. If you do that any more, we
may not come back for you." As children of six or seven show
interest in their sexual parts or those of another child, parents
can humiliate them by their ridicule: "God did not mean for
you to play with that. If he had, he would have made a toy of
it. Stop that foolishness!" As adolescents begin dating, they
may be admonished, "Whatever you do when you are on a
date, just be sure it is something that Jesus can return at any
time and find you doing!" These responses are thinly veiled
verbal abuse in religious garb. Moreover, parents saturated
with religiosity may not be consistent. They may act in private
with their children in a harsh, vindictive way that is completely
dissociated from their other "religious" personality. The important exclusion is the absence of any portrayal of God as
loving, cherishing, and caring for each child. Similarly, the
parents' own arrogance and lack of awareness of their human
shortcomings is evident.

One of the greatest services that can be rendered by the
teaching and preaching ministries of the church—combined
with small-group recovery ministries to abused children and
adults—is to challenge this kind of abuse by challenging the
kind of gospel being taught and preached. We can raise the
consciousness of congregations and create and inform their
conscience about the damage to the "capacity for commitment" to Christ and his church that such abuse inflicts. In the
avoidant person, we find ourselves considering the most fragile of the disordered personalities yet discussed. As we do so,
we move from the work of the physician, to the work of teachers in and out of the church, to the kind of care parents give
children at home. Such a study creates a renewed sense of
mission for the church in the social order of justice, mercy,
and a humble walk with God.

8

Persons on the Edge of Chaos

The patterns of difficulties in living we have considered so far are indeed "ways of life" for many. In reviewing these ways of life, we can discern defective child-rearing practices that set the pattern. As Christians concerned with the influence of ethical guidance and the maturation of troubled persons, we can see fairly clear evidence of self-centeredness, exploitation of other people, the abuse of children and youth, and the irresponsibility of emerging adults in shouldering their part of the load of being human. These call for an agonizing reappraisal of the ministry of the churches today. Furthermore, as we have considered these personality disorders, we have seen that individual, group, and community teaching, counseling, psychotherapy, and discipline in ethical decision-making are the main treatment resources. Only to a limited extent are specific uses of psychiatric medications the treatments of choice.

Moreover, formal religious influences have generally left these underlying formations of personality untouched. Religious behavior has taken the form of the personality disorder more often than religious experience has wrought a deep change in the patterns of this disorder. In short, the person's basic way of life continues as it was. The mass approaches to religion, as well as the mass approaches to the rest of the education of the individual, lacked the power of personal confrontation, the concern with transformation, or the wisdom needed to discern that anything was really out of the ordinary.

In fact, in considering the ways of life named thus far, we regularly were troubled to see that they are held up as worthy models to be copied and as necessary for "getting somewhere" in our competitive and acquisitive American culture.

As for the physicians who have written most perceptively about these personality disorders—including Millon, Fromm, Horney, Freud, Sullivan, and Erikson, among many others—we have found them to be just as concerned about the kind of culture that produces the disorders as they are about diagnosing and treating what Karen Horney called "the neurotic personality of *our time*" (italics mine).

These *are* times that try people's souls. The foregoing pages epitomize how souls are tried and how "all we like sheep have gone astray; we have turned every one to his own way; and the LORD has laid on him the iniquity of us all." The Lord Jesus Christ's suffering is not just for this, that, or the other errant sheep. His redemption calls all of us corporately to a severe mercy in the face of our responsibility as a people for our times. As a colleague once told me, "Unless we come to terms as a Christian community with the cultural arson that destroys individuals and homes, pastoral counseling, psychotherapy, and psychiatry will continue to be the fire department of churches." If we changed the metaphor to a medical one, we could say, "Until we clear the swamps of mosquitoes, we will continue to have epidemics of malaria."

Personalities on the Edge of Chaos

In this chapter we will consider three different kinds of "severe" personality disorders, as Theodore Millon calls them. Their plights of existence are indeed "ways of life," but those who experience them live their lives on the edge of the primeval chaos of psychotic schisms from the most minimal realities of everyday life. These disorders more often develop into acute episodes of severe emotional illness and need both emergency and extended psychiatric treatment. They are the least accessible to pastoral counseling and to any form of psychotherapy. They seem to me to need a community of care that schools and churches fall short of, and hospitals and correctional institutions are only temporarily and palliatively helpful.

These personality disorders are described in DSM III as the borderline personality (the "stably unstable"), the paranoid personality (the "suspicious"), and the schizotypal personality (the "eccentric" or "odd"). A profile of each of these will help differentiate them somewhat from one another. Then a composite profile of the features they have in common will form the basis for considering our responsibilities and opportunities for relating to them and caring for them.

The Borderline or "Stably Unstable" Personality

A considerable number of physicians feel that this diagnostic label is one of the most abused terms in the field of psychiatry. They feel that it is misused as a foil for the hostility of the physician toward a difficult patient, as a catchall diagnosis for "sloppy and imprecise diagnostic thinking," as an excuse for mistakes in treatment or acting-out against the person (Reiser and Levenson 1984).

However, careful assessment reflects that borderline personalities are lastingly unstable individuals. They have repeated false starts and failures in school, work, and marriage. Most significantly, they have repeated brief but reversible psychotic episodes. They are severely impulsive in such acts as spending, sex, gambling, substance abuse, shoplifting, overeating, or physically hurting themselves. Their outbursts of intense anger and their lack of control are frequent and inappropriate.

More seriously than this, they have severe identity confusion as to who they are and what they are supposed to be or to become. They have turbulent shifts of mood from depression to anxiety to irritability and rage, usually lasting from a few hours to a few days, with as quick a return to a normal mood. They are intolerant of being alone and frantically try to find someone to be with so they will not become depressed. They regard their lives as chronically empty and boring.

In the context of a church or a school, these persons will have many people to whom they frantically appeal. There may be from two to fifteen or twenty people who are seeking to "help" them. These people get acquainted with each other, and a recurrent topic of conversation is this one person and his or her latest episodes of terror, be they self-mutilations, suicidal gestures, accidents, or fights.

In their religious thought, borderline persons present as much confusion about the presence and nature of God as they do about their own identity and purpose. They complain that their prayers are empty and that God is never near them. Making a connection between their somewhat nominal, mechanical involvement in the church and their personal serenity draws a blank expression and a poverty of thought and response. The main meaning they draw from church life is that there are numerous people who protect them from being alone, a thing of which they are terrified. When they become frantic about being alone, several people in a congregation will be called in rapid succession. From three to ten people will be actively seeking to get the person hospitalized for fear that—for example—he may hurt himself in an automobile accident, or she may make a suicide attempt or at least plead that someone come and be with her. Often, when they have been hospitalized such persons "clear up" in three to five days. The whole group of those who went through the crisis gradually gets exhausted after several of these episodes. The spiritual dilemma of caring for these persons is knowing how to be a steadfast, sustaining person and at the same time maintain realistic but considerate limits on their demanding natures. How can one portray the compassion and wisdom of the Lord Jesus Christ and at the same time set realistic limits on such impulsive expectations?

The Suspicious or Paranoid Personality

Although there are notable exceptions among the population of people who live suspicious, paranoid lives of combined grandiosity and expectation of persecution, most of them are viewed by others as hostile, stubborn, and defensive. Occasionally they will be viewed as very sharp observers who are energetic, ambitious, and capable. These latter persons have a "headline intelligence" that picks up on "in" phrases, catchwords, and the headlines of current events and uses them to brandish their grandiose self-estimates. However, if pushed for the details of such subjects, they have not read the fine print of whatever topic they raise. They are very conscious of power systems and rank people according to whether they are inferior or superior.

As in the case of borderline personalities, paranoid persons ordinarily are not perceived as having, nor do they in fact attain, much stability in school, marriage, or work experiences. Similarly also, they are characterized by periodic brief psychotic episodes fraught with irrational actions and delusional thought patterns. Hence they are repeatedly in need of psychiatric help on a short-term crisis-intervention basis.

Since adolescence these persons have been vigilantly mistrustful. They anticipate criticism and deception in a much more crafty way than do avoidant persons. Envy and jealousy are their deadly besetting sins. Their mistrust pushes them into argumentative situations in which they are fractious and constantly rubbing other people the wrong way and putting them down. They take extremely trivial events and exaggerate them to build a grandiose picture of their accomplishments. They view peripheral and inconsequential remarks and happenings as having hidden meanings and as being critical of themselves. As Millon says, for these persons "little difference exists between what they have seen and what they have thought. . . . Chains of unconnected facts are fitted together. An inexorable course from imagination to supposition to suspicion takes place and soon a system of invalid and unshakable beliefs has been created" (1981:381).

From a religious point of view, DSM III (p. 308) makes an important observation about the paranoid personality:

> This disorder rarely comes to clinical attention, since such persons rarely seek help for their personality problems or require hospitalization. Owing to a tendency of some of them to be moralistic, grandiose, and extrapunitive, it seems likely that the individuals with this disorder are overrepresented among leaders of mystical or esoteric religions and of pseudoscientific and quasi-political groups.

Earlier I suggested that the authoritarian religious leader is predominantly narcissistic. However, the grandiosity of the paranoid personality is saturated with narcissism. Hugo G. Zee says this in a discussion of the Guyana massacre-by-suicide of Jim Jones and his followers. Jones's history is revealing. He was born near Lynn, Indiana, in 1931, at a time when casket-making was the major industry of the town. His father was a disabled World War II veteran and an active member of the Ku Klux Klan. His mother repeatedly dreamed of her dead mother. In one of the dreams the older woman prophesied that the daughter would bear a son who would right the wrongs of the world. She became convinced that her son would be a messiah. When Jim Jones was fourteen his parents separated and six years later his father died. His mother lived until just before Jim Jones's own death.

Jones began preaching shortly after his parents were divorced, when he was fourteen. Remarkably enough, this son of a Ku Klux Klan devotee began preaching to a black church. He formed his ministerial career in the mainline Methodist Church. Yet he soon dropped out of any schooling beyond high school. He abandoned the Methodist Church as a "loveless" church. He married a woman much older and better educated then he. The story of his life, says Zee, is one of betrayal of his father, his hometown, his Methodist relationship, his wife, his allegiance to the Christian faith, his government, his country, and finally his own followers. Zee says that this pattern of betrayal is a major feature of paranoid personalities. Jones finally denounced the Bible and dramatically spit upon it, telling his followers they paid too much attention to it and not to him. He died convinced that "they," a government conspiracy, were out to get him and would torture and kill him and his followers. (See Zee 1980:345–363.)

This bizarre case documents the DSM III observation about the moralistic and grandiose ideation of the paranoid personality appearing in certain kinds of religious leaders. However, paranoid leadership appears in much less bizarre church situations within mainline religious groups.

For example, some pastors are in perpetual conflict with contending groups in the churches. Under normal leadership, these conflicts can be faced, assessed, and resolved and the congregation gets on with its main purpose of teaching, preaching, and caring for persons. However, in my own consultation work I have seen pastors who repeatedly are involved in forming a splinter group of loyal followers, pulling out of the mainline church and forming a new church built around the pastor as the final voice in all decisions. In one instance, a pastor created such schisms in four successive churches. In the last of these splits, the group loyal to him in turn was torn apart with controversy.

This same set of dynamics works with larger denominational groups when exhibitionistic, grandiose leaders move to take over the power structure of a denomination. Greed, envy, jealousy, accusations of disloyalty, expectation of trickery, hypervigilant scanning of the work of the denomination for signs of threat, secretive guardedness, and overconcern with hidden motives and special meanings in what is being said and done are evident. Any sense of humor goes out of the fellowship as the atmosphere itself becomes more and more paranoid. Great pride is taken in being objective, rational, and unemotional. Feelings of tenderness, gentleness, and warmth disappear. The paranoid personality of the leader sours the atmosphere of the denomination. These people fill the air with the radioactive fallout of their suspicions.

The Schizotypal or Eccentric Personality

In this third disturbing personality disorder, once again we are dealing with persons whose grasp of reality is very shaky indeed. They live on the edge of the chaos of brief but hectic psychotic episodes. Also, they are their own worst enemies in creating their own setbacks in scholastic, marital, and work pursuits.

The schizotypal personality can be literally saturated with

a superstitious religion of magic that seems odd and eccentric to the conventionally religious person and the person for whom religion also is a matter of common sense. For example, he or she may say, "I cut my finger off and God is growing it back." "I saw God this morning running along a tree limb. He was a bird. He sang to me." "God helps me to read other people's minds, and I know ahead of time when things are going to happen. They happen and I can say, I told you so."

The speech pattern of schizotypal persons is odd. They will start to tell you one thing, then digress into something else and go into a labyrinth of detail that has little or nothing to do with the original topic. You become increasingly uncomfortable on their behalf, but they are lost in their own jumbled collage of detail.

These persons suffer illusions of the presence of "forces" or persons not actually present; for example, they may talk with or write letters to persons who are dead. They become depersonalized, uncertain as to who they are, and are thrown into panic attacks.

In face-to-face conversation with you, they are aloof and cold and you are likely to sense them as being out of it and far away. You may find that their general eccentricity shows up in the odd way they dress and sit, in their posture, and in their strangeness at a church dinner with their awkward and bizarre table manners.

The overall impression you have of schizotypal personalities is that they are isolated, have few friends, and limit their social contacts to the barest essentials of work, church life, and so on. Indeed, they are lonely people, but you may feel this *for* them more than they seem to mind it themselves. Every church to which I have been related has a persistent population of these quaint, odd, lonely people. A congregation simply moves over and makes room for them and lets them go along for the ride in whatever activities they attend.

DSM III makes the observation that schizotypal personalities "are prone to eccentric convictions, such as bigotry and fringe religious beliefs." One such person I knew in a rural parish was a man who had the eccentric belief that his interpretation of the Bible was the only one he would permit his wife and children to hear. He kept them in, held church in his home, baptized them himself, and permitted no one to "contaminate their minds." Wandering street prophets in large cities present bigoted beliefs and appeal for a following in a setting where they are most assured they will not get any following to bother them.

Common Problems of Borderline, Paranoid, and Schizotypal Personalities

Theodore Millon described in some detail three common features among these three personality disorders: developmental immaturity or social invalidism, cognitive disorganization or a deep thought disorder, and feelings of estrangement or alienation. In periods of high crisis, they will develop "transient psychotic symptoms," according to DSM III. The tragedy occurs, says Millon, "perhaps because of poor hospital management or unreceptive family conditions—these patients remain hospitalized only to disintegrate progressively into more pervasive and enduring pathological patterns. Isolated increasingly from normal social activities and having acquired the habits and rewards of hospital life, they give up the efforts to regain a meaningful 'outside' existence and allow themselves to slip into the emptiness of permanent decompensation" (Millon 1981:330–331).

In my clinical care of these personalities in the context of churches and schools as well as hospitals, I can add other commonalities they share.

They share a common high and persistent level of "nuisance" to those with whom they live and work. What to other people are the ordinary stresses of everyday living become major catastrophes to them. They can use up elaborate quantities of time, energy, attention, and even money in trying to make life possible with them and for them. For example, a fifty-year-old woman who is harmless and is no danger to herself or other people nevertheless can become an outrage in a small town. She can do so by going from restaurant to restaurant, sitting down by people who are eating their meal, talking with them, and as she is talking with them eat from their plates! This is a public nuisance.

Again, as I have indicated before, such persons have a way of getting many counselors, physicians, social caseworkers, teachers, professors, and deans involved in helping them. They become agitated at times of severe stress, and many times this is when all their helpers are also under stress. For example, a student is likely to decompensate when final exams or commencement approaches. Everybody is under stress at such a time. Yet these persons do not become a part of the "community of suffering." They isolate themselves, develop strange and bizarre behaviors, and require all-out assistance over and above the line of duty from others around them.

Another characteristic these persons share is that they quite often have no place of their own "to be" and no place to go where they are safe. Exhausted relatives do not want them, the hospital is both expensive and habit-forming, and churches do not have dormitories. Many times they stay in school with no particular place to go or purpose for being there until they wear out their welcome. Their alienation is both individually intense and intensified by the community. There is no institution adapted to their needs. In the days of large state hospitals with huge farms to be operated by patients in what was called "industrial therapy," the simplified life of a farm gave them both the distance and the structure where they could "be." These people are overrepresented in the population of homeless street people, especially in these times of deinstitutionalization of mentally ill persons. In an earlier time these drifters from place to place were called "hobo" personalities.

Special Challenges of the Christian Community

Being Prepared for the Worst

The exceptional vulnerability of these persons to falling apart or disintegrating into psychotic states means that the staff and membership of a church must be prepared for that to happen. Inasmuch as these breakdowns occur when persons are under stress, one way to be prepared is to watch for impending crises in their lives. Many of these crises are developmental and can be predicted, such as the beginning and end of a school year, plans for a marriage, expecting a child to be born, or the anticipation of the death of a parent or spouse after a lingering illness. Even though these persons do not of their own accord seek the specialized care of a physician, the ministers and the membership of a church can naturally and appropriately intervene at these crisis times. The loss of a job, separation from a mate, divorce, and other such crises are times when the person is most open to a note of sympathy, and a telephone call of concern or a visit to their residence is not only appropriate but often expected by them. This is an advantage the church and its ministers have over physicians, except in rare instances.

However, once an intervention has taken place and you or I find that the person is already coming apart at the seams in a psychotic episode, a physician is needed immediately. One good way of being prepared for this is to have close working relationships with physicians within the church membership and beyond the walls of the church as well. If you and I are known quantities, even trusted friends of these physicians, we are all the more prepared to care for these persons in an acute decompensation into psychosis. We can be ministers of introduction, acting as a liaison between the ill person and the physician. We can even accompany them, if they will permit it, as they go to the doctor.

Making Provision for a "Place to Be"

After brief hospitalization, the critical issue is where such people will live. Sometimes the family is exhausted and fed up with the repeated breakdowns. In many instances the person will have no family. Social agencies in large communities may have halfway houses, group homes, in which such persons can be in transitional care pending their becoming more independent in their living.

The churches themselves in a few instances see the need for a "place to be" for persons who are too vulnerable to stay in a school or at home and yet will not thrive in long hospital stays. The Trinity Baptist Church in Lexington, Kentucky, saw a need for a special Sunday school class for adult mentally retarded persons. As the word got around the community, the class grew to eighty persons who attended regularly. Then a class member's parents, both mother and father, died in the same general span of time. The church initiated a fund-raising drive and bought a working farm. A couple who had been working with the Sunday school class made a mid-life career change and the church employed them to supervise a group home and work opportunity on the farm for the adult sons and daughters of mentally retarded persons. Now the Quest Farm is in full operation.

It seems reasonable, then, that the churches should consider the need of people with such fragile mental stability for a place to be and work to do as an option for their outreach ministry. These persons have the same residual problems of placeless, purposeful, worklessness, and loneliness as do schizophrenic and psychotically depressed people. Psychiatry does an increasingly effective job of clearing up the symptoms of psychoses, but is in need of the kind of compassion and down-to-earth commitment that the Trinity Baptist Church in Lexington demonstrates in follow-up care for seriously disturbed mentally ill persons, also.

Reinterpreting Christian Calling and Vocation

The Christian community is caught up in the human struggle of persons for meaningful purpose, caring relationships, and a strong sense of identity and direction of their lives under God. Christian experience involves all of this. John Bunyan wrote the story of his own struggles of the soul in finding the City of God. Then he wrote another story of how his wife and family found their way safely there as well.

The church touches a vocational nerve in people's lives at many points—in the struggle of a child or young person to be competent in school, in the choice of a mate and the decision to be married, in marriage and family counseling of troubled families, in parent-child problems, and in the many decisions people make about their work. The great deficits of all the personality disorders appear most vividly at these points. The decompensations of the more malignant of the personality disorders tend to appear at these points. Therefore, a quiet, patient, persistent quest to know the mind and purpose of God for their lives, sustained and enriched by the assurance that these persons are beloved children of God, who has a meaning, a purpose, a place, and a loving use for them, is the overall strategy of our care for them. Whatever God has called them to be and become, he does not intend that they be permanent mental patients. He intends that they unearth and invest their unique gifts. We are a steadfast community of faith questing with them for those gifts. We are a community of encouragement and celebration with them as they get their lives together in God's presence.

9

After the Masks
Are Gone

The whole conversation thus far has been about *dis*orders of personality. With the exception of the borderline, the paranoid, and the schizotypal, these disorders are ways of life the person has learned to reenact in adult life. They do not seem to involve specific abnormalities in the central nervous system or other organ systems of the body. Psychiatrists do not ordinarily consider these disorders in living as requiring the use of psychotropic medications. They have little opportunity to do psychotherapy with such persons because these persons seldom see the necessity for insight, understanding, or instruction. Unteachability runs these persons aground in the troubled waters of home, school, marriage, workplace, and church. Yet that very unteachability—which can be translated "hardness of heart"—began in the long-standing teaching by which they learned some things about themselves and the world that now call for unlearning.

One of the greatest tributes that can be paid to a parent, a teacher, a physician, a pastor, or anyone else who influences, instructs, and guides other people is that this person never taught a given individual something he or she had to unlearn. Yet as we have studied the different personality disorders, we have unmasked deep-seated, unhealthy attitudes and convictions that people have been taught at home, in the school, in the church, and in the culture of narcissism, competition, and power in which they and we live and work. Second Timothy 4:3 tells us that "the time is coming when people will not endure sound teaching." Remarkably, the word "sound" is translated from the Greek *hygiainousēs,* a form of the word from which we get "hygiene," the science of maintaining health.

Therefore, in this chapter let us concentrate on the kind of teaching, nurture, and discerning love that creates ordered rather than disordered personalities among the people of God.

Some Meanings of Order

Sometimes when you use the word "order," you are simply asking for something—as when the waiter or waitress takes your order in a restaurant. At other times, you add force to the word and are commanding someone, as when you order subordinates to do something. Pilate ordered that the body of Jesus be given to Joseph of Arimathea (Matt. 27:58). This meaning of order is found in the New Testament. However, it is not the meaning we have in mind when it comes to providing health-giving teachings so that ordered personalities will be the result, rather than disordered ones. The New Testament has other meanings of order that are much more significant for our understanding and action.

First Timothy 1:4–5 uses the word *oikonomia* to describe the divine order, teaching, or stewardship that is characterized by "love that issues from a pure heart and a good conscience and sincere faith." The apostle Paul in referring to glossolalia in the church says, "Do not forbid speaking in tongues; but all things should be done decently and in order" (1 Cor. 14:39b–40). Paul's use of the words *kata taxin* (in order) may well be a military figure of speech that refers to staying in line and not turning a well-ordered regiment into a disorderly mob. However, Robertson and Plummer (1953:328) interpret it to mean ecclesiastical decorum or behavior. They say that "beauty and harmony prevail in God's universe, where each part discharges its proper function without slackness or encroachment; and beauty and harmony prevail in the worship of God." The churches have made much of order in worship, and even more of the order of salvation. Much energy is spent in the ordering of the Christian experience of the growing individual through either the sacraments of the liturgical churches or the ordinances of the churches who make much of spontaneity and little of order. Nevertheless, a programmatic order of salvation exists through which a person must move or be moved for redemption in Jesus Christ.

However, there is a word for order used in one of Jesus' parables that gets closest to our concern for the ordered personality: it is *kosmeō*. Jesus had just cast out a demon that was dumb, and when he did so, the dumb man spoke. The people were amazed, and some of them accused him of being

in league with Beelzebul. He replied that a house divided
against itself could not stand and told them this parable:

> When the unclean spirit has gone out of a man, he passes
> through waterless places seeking rest; and finding none he
> says, "I will return to my house from which I came." And when
> he comes he finds it swept and put in order. Then he goes and
> brings seven more spirits more evil than himself, and they
> enter and dwell there; and the last state of that man becomes
> worse than the first. (Luke 11:24–26)

The house was "put in order." The word thus translated,
kosmeō, means literally "to adorn and decorate," as is more
vividly illustrated in Revelation 21:2, where John envisions
the new Jerusalem "coming down out of heaven from God,
prepared as a bride adorned for her husband." In its metaphorical sense, *kosmeō* means to make your whole personality
abundantly beautiful and spiritually attractive. Jesus seems to
be saying that the person who was convalescing from the
ravages of an unclean spirit needs further attention than the
mere casting out of the spirit. The rest of the being needs
total care. Today we know that merely to remove the un-
wholesome symptoms of the psychotic regressions of a person suffering with a lifelong personality disorder, without
attention to the whole system of the "house" they live in, is
to invite seven times as much trouble. The system itself is in
need of change. The people in that system—in addition to the
identifiable patient—who are not with us in making those
changes are against us and the patient. When Jesus spoke as
a healer in the instance cited here, he was as concerned with
the spiritual atmosphere of the system in which the dumb man
lived as he was with what he himself saw as the precarious
situation of a house "swept and put in order" standing empty.
The emptiness of the house spoke volumes. The ordered
personality stays at risk when it is empty of meaning, purpose,
vocation, and a genuine sense of personal worth derived from
God and blessed by the fellowship of family and of faith.

Character and the Ordered Personality

When psychiatrists speak of personality disorders less formally than in DSM III, in books such as Millon's definitive
volume, and in journal articles, they use the term "character
disorders." However, with the exception of a few psy-
choanalysts they do not give a clear definition of what they
mean by "character." The same could be said of their use of

the word "reality." One of the best definitions is found in
Hinsie and Campbell's *Psychiatric Dictionary* (1970:120):

> *Character* in current usage [is] approximately equivalent to *per-
> sonality.* . . . It includes the characteristic (and to some extent
> predictable) behavior-response patterns that each person
> evolves, both consciously and unconsciously, as his style of life
> or way of being in adapting to his environment and main-
> taining a stable, reciprocal relationship with human and
> non-human environment. . . . It must be recognized that any
> diagnosis of *character disorder or personality disturbance* is funda-
> mentally a social diagnosis and made by other people than the
> subject himself, whose behavior is perceived by others as de-
> structive, frightening, nonconforming, or otherwise deviant.

The phrases "other people" and "social diagnosis" suggest
that parents and siblings, schoolmates and teachers, lovers
and spouses, co-workers and employers, church members
and ministers, and police authorities are the primary diagnosticians and have final responsibility for treatment of persons
whom they deem to have a character disorder. In brief, the
community becomes both diagnostician and therapist. The
irony of this is that the community—the family, the school, the
church, the places of work, and the maintainers of law and
civil order—are at the same time the makers, shapers, ar-
chitects, engineers, and builders of the characters they diag-
nose and treat. All of us need to go back to the drawing
boards and see whether the intention of the Author and Creator of us all has informed our work. If so, have we acted in
accord with that intention?

When we turn to the New Testament for an understanding
of character, we find the beginnings of answers to this last
question. Hebrews 1:3 states that Jesus the Christ "reflects
the glory of God and bears the very stamp of his nature,
upholding the universe by his word of power." The words
"very stamp" translate the Greek word *charactēr.* This is a
much more existential and less behavioral understanding of
character than the psychiatric definition. Character is the
shape of the very being of a person, not just external behavior. Behavior expresses this being, this nature. The book of
Hebrews uses another word, *ametatheton,* which is translated
"unchangeable character" (Heb. 6:17), to describe the character of God's purpose. In many persons suffering from character disorders we discovered a fickleness of purpose at best,
an absence of purpose at worst, and a lack of the steadfastness
or unchangeableness of a high calling in their lives.

Such a high calling would challenge us to undergo stress and forgo immediate satisfactions in behalf of that calling. The apostle Paul uses another word for character in Romans 5:4, *dokimē*. In the suffering of life, he says, we can rejoice in knowing that "suffering produces endurance, and endurance produces character, and character produces hope, and hope does not disappoint us, because God's love has been poured into our hearts through the Holy Spirit which has been given to us." Endurance puts a person to the test, and the outcome is character. Character is not an inert, sterile entity. Character actively works to generate hope. Suffering is a sort of test run of endurance to generate character. In personal relationships, Paul tested the character of people. He uses *dokimē* in this sense in 2 Corinthians 2:9: "For this is why I wrote, that I might test you and know whether you are obedient in everything."

Character, then, is that "stamp" of our very nature that is etched there by our having endured the tests of frustration and suffering and accepted the disciplines of obedience to the calling of God in Jesus Christ.

In our study of personality or character disorders, one way of differentiating them is to ask, What is the locus or center of their patterns of obedience? For example, dependent persons center their obedience on the directives, cues, and nurturance of other people. Narcissistic personalities are obedient only to their self-absorbed wishes and grandiose self-image. Compulsive persons have an "unnecessary conscience" of scrupulosity as the locus of their drivenness.

We could generalize and say that the personality is *disordered* by the defective character of the habitual center or locus of the personal energies of a person. The ordering of personality begins with the testing of the character of these habitual centerings of the being of the person. This testing is what the teachings of Jesus and the prophets aim to do.

The Formation and Transformation of the Order and Disorder of the Christian Person

A general consensus seems to have emerged in the psychiatric community that personality disorders are the long-term way of life, or scheme of existence, of individuals. They have been formed in initial and continuing family interactions. The formal education of the person ordinarily does not challenge this formation in any specific way, but simply works around it. The ritual life of such an individual's religious participation tends to be schematized along the lines of the particular disorder. Occasionally through the radical transformation of a crisis conversion the personality is reordered. As we look at the New Testament teachings, we find some fresh light on the intention of God in the formation and transformation of the poignant disorders of our lives.

May Christ Be Formed in You!

The apostle Paul in writing to the Galatians was appalled. They had been "bewitched" and seduced by the legalists into believing that they were bound to the legalisms of the Jewish law in order to be acceptable to Christ. They had returned to their compulsive way of life and were living under this addiction. He told them that it was as if he were in the travail or labor of birth himself in his desire for the transformation of their lives. He would be in travail, he said, until "Christ is formed in you" (Gal. 4:19). The Greek word he used is very familiar to us: *morphothē*, from *morphein*, "to form, to shape." It is a metaphor or symbol of the formation of an embryo. He calls them "my little children." He pictures himself in a feminine role as having birthed them in Christ. Now he is having to go through the process *again* until Christ is formed in them.

This is the poignant plight of the individual whose Christian experience has been so superficial that a radical rebirth is in order so that Christ may be formed within them. They change the lifelong scheme which they have brought from their earthly family and which has continued in spite of what Christ has done for them. Earlier, in Galatians 2:20, Paul stated more specifically what he meant by Christ being formed in us: "I have been crucified with Christ; it is no longer I who live, but Christ who lives in me; and the life I now live in the flesh I live by faith in the Son of God, who loved me and gave himself for me."

Through the process of the organization, growth, and development of a religious fellowship, the initial strength of the teachings of the group is gradually diminished. The transmission of those teachings through the parent-child relationship is increasingly dominated by the kind of relationship going on between the parents and the children. Tradition, ritual, and church routine replace the immediacy and the radiance of the transforming power of the presence of Christ being formed in the believer. It is little wonder then that the very substance of the gospel as personal participation of the individual and the group in the crucifixion, burial, and resurrection of Christ whereby Christ is formed within them becomes either a doctrine or a ritual such as baptism. Persons can go through the motions and be untouched and unchanged in the personality disorders they bring to their baptism. Their particular disordered way of relating to persons—other church members, spouse, employer, God—goes untouched at best; at worst, they are given a spurious sense that their dependency, narcissism, negativism, manipulativeness, and detachment have divine sanction and they may do as they please in God's name.

This gloomy picture, however, is not the way it has to be or always turns out to be. Throughout our discussion of each of the ways of life we call personality disorders, I have observed that people are caused to stop, look, listen, question, and reconsider their life when faced with crises of inalterable situations, when caught in the web of human circumstance that their way of life has woven. These crises can be a job failure, a marriage failure, the death of a parent who has kept the faulty organization somewhat functional, being convicted of a felony and imprisoned at the peak of imagined success, or any of the thousand mortal ills to which human flesh is heir. These crises can be the individual's response to massive social calamities such as the Great Depression, World War II, the Vietnam War, or the present wave of bankruptcies and farm foreclosures.

James Loder has called such events "convictional experiences"(1981:180). Others have called them a person's "being thrown off balance" in his or her accustomed way of living. These can become teachable moments. In the words of William Carey, man's extremity becomes God's opportunity. In human life we each live our own particular way of life, our particular disordered existence. This disordered existence has a tether or chain of a certain length in terms both of time and of other people's patience. For us this tether is the DNA chain that preordains our bodily health, the limits our heritage built into us, and the inherent limitations of being human that in creation God set for all of us. These disruptions in our knowing context, these times of being thrown off balance, serve to let us know that we have come to the end of our tether. Our extremity becomes God's opportunity. We either change radically or, having learned nothing from the teachable moment, we continue to wander in the misty flats of our own self-centeredness. The telling difference is made by the degree of openness and teachability with which we go through being thrown off balance in the rupturing of our knowing context.

The definable personality disorders bear psychological markers of the person's lack of insight, lack of foresight, and unwillingness to appoint or ordain any other person as his or her teacher. Relatives will complain, "Nobody can tell him [her] anything." In Jesus' discussion of marital breakdowns and divorce, he said this was "for your hardness of heart"—or, as the *Good News Bible* translates, "because you are so hard to teach." Proverbs 2:1–5 makes this appeal:

> My son, if you receive my words
>   and treasure up my commandments with you,
> making your ear attentive to wisdom
>   and inclining your heart to understanding;
> yes, if you cry out for insight
>   and raise your voice for understanding,
> if you seek it like silver
>   and search for it as for hidden treasures;
> then you will understand the fear of the LORD
>   and find the knowledge of God.

The mass-production assembly lines both of organized denominations and of media-centered religious propaganda do not seem to lend themselves to valuing very highly the "crying out for insight" and "raising your voice for understanding" which the writer of Proverbs commends as prerequisites for understanding the fear of the Lord and finding the knowledge of God. In this as the fellowship of believers in Christ, given the gift of discernment by the Holy Spirit, we are primarily responsible. It is the leaven we have to offer to the whole lump of human life. It is the salt with which God through us makes life possible and palatable. It is the light we dare not put under a bushel at the risk of becoming stale, tiring, boring, and useless in the transformation of human lives. The fear of God, the knowledge of God, and the wisdom of God are like silver, like hidden treasure. In this we are called to be competent.

However, we have taken on another preoccupation that pushes us beyond the arena of our competency. That preoccupation is the corporate business model for both the churches and the secondary institutions such as schools, seminaries, hospitals, nursing homes, and retirement centers. The order of salvation, whether it be a sacramental system, steps in order to be saved, or the religious revival, becomes instead a recruitment technique that we use to build bigger and bigger churches, cathedrals, and denominations. We do this at a time when the corporate businesses of our country are in great trouble for expanding themselves beyond the level of their original competence. As Robert J. Samuelson (1986:45) says,

> They tend to expand to the level of their incompetence and inefficiency. There's a crude cycle of growth and decay. Corporate success sows the seeds for future failure. Successful companies strive to do more and get bigger. But this striving makes firms unwieldy or prompts them to diversify into areas where they are inept. These mistakes make the companies less efficient; . . . their ambitions made the companies increasingly unmanageable.

Religious groups build towers of Babel to "make a name for themselves." Religious competition to be bigger and bigger is no exception to the process of decay. Apropos of our central concern for the transformation of personality disorders, another thing happens in this adoption of the corporate model for churches. The crude cycle of growth and decay happens to churches as a result of our misguided ambitions. These tend to glorify some of the personality disorders such as the aggressive antisocial way of life, the grandiose paranoid way of life, and the self-absorbed narcissistic way of life. At the same time, they tend to exploit persons laboring under the weight of other personality disorders such as the dependent, the histrionic, and the compulsive ways of life. Thus churches ignore or trample underfoot in ambitious haste persons who are asocial, avoidant, and stably unstable. They have no use for them. The search for divine wisdom that transforms the disorder of a person into a "divine order" is forsaken in behalf of show business. As Bill Moyers, when he resigned as a newsman from CBS television, said of company policy, "Instead of the role of gathering, weighing, sorting and explaining the flux of events and issues, we began to be influenced by the desire first to please the audience. The object was to 'hook' them by pretending this was not news at all. . . . Once you decide to titillate instead of illuminate you are on a slippery slope" (*Courier-Journal*, Louisville, Ky., September 17, 1986, p. A-13).

An analogous situation exists in the religious community. As Isaiah said:

> For they are a rebellious people,
>   lying sons,
> sons who will not hear
>   the instruction of the LORD;

who say to the seers, "See not";
   and to the prophets,
      "Prophesy not to us what is right; speak to us
      smooth things,
   prophesy illusions,
leave the way, turn aside from the path,
   let us hear no more of the Holy One of Israel."
                                           (Isa. 30:9–11)

The end result of these responses of the churches of today is vividly portrayed in John Bunyan's *Pilgrim's Progress*. Christian comes to a town, the name of which is Vanity. A fair is kept there, "called Vanity Fair, because the town where it is kept is lighter than vanity, also because all that is sold there or cometh there is vanity. . . . This fair is no new erected business, but a thing of ancient standing." Bunyan says that our Lord Jesus Christ

> went through this town to his own country, and that upon a fair-day too. . . . Beelzebub, the chief lord of this fair . . . invited him to buy of his vanities, yea, would have made him lord of the fair, would he but have done him reverence as he went through the town. Yea, because he was such a person of honor, Beelzebub had him from street to street, and showed him all the kingdoms of the world in a little time, that he might, if possible, allure the Blessed One to [bargain for] and buy some of his vanities; but he had no mind to the merchandise, and, therefore, left the town without laying out so much as one farthing upon these vanities.

The same issue prevails in the power pyramids of today's religious Vanity Fair.

However, the cryptic ethical, spiritual, and cultural issues folded into the psychiatric descriptions of the attitudes of persons with personality disorders give the discerning Christian community a prophetic realism about our mission. This prophetic realism cuts away the Vanity Fair of the desire to become a religious "superpower." God is not a God of confusion, but this self-elevation is such a god. At both the corporate and personal levels of the life of Christians, Paul's appeal to the Romans provides the biblical basis for a new agenda for churches to take up afresh the central competency given to us by the Lord Jesus Christ:

> So then, my brothers, because of God's great mercy to us I appeal to you: Offer yourselves as a living sacrifice to God, dedicated to his service and pleasing to him. This is the true worship that you should offer. Do not conform yourselves to

the standards of this world, but let God transform you inwardly by a complete change of your mind. Then you will be able to know the will of God—what is good and is pleasing to him and is perfect. (Rom. 12:1–2, TEV)

A complete change of your mind is a new ordering of the whole personality. Such an ordering is the work of God, brought out of the chaos in a new creation. As Cranfield interprets this passage (1979:607): "The transformation is not something which is brought about in an instant; . . . it is a process which has to go on all the time in the Christian in this life."

I would interpret this process as one in which you and I appoint the Lord Jesus Christ as our Teacher. We bring the disordered schemata of our lives under the scrutiny of his instruction. As I have said, the person with a personality disorder internally resists letting anyone be his or her teacher. A profound fear energizes this resistance. The love of God in Jesus Christ casts out this fear. Thus we *let* God transform our minds as we present ourselves to God and enroll ourselves in the instruction of Jesus Christ, his Son. Through this process of reordering our lives, the transformation happens. "And we all, with unveiled face, beholding the glory of the Lord, are being changed into his likeness from one degree of glory to another; for this comes from the Lord who is the Spirit" (2 Cor. 3:18).

As we review the schemata or life-styles or ways of life of the different personality disorders, we can become quite specific about the crucial concerns for the transforming and ordering of life which they all tend to raise. These crucial concerns are imperatives for the work of Jesus Christ, once he has been accepted and appointed as Teacher. His imperatives become the primary issues for the teaching ministry of a fellowship of believers in him. As Kierkegaard (1946:296) says, this instruction does not promise that a person can be "catechized and congratulated in the space of an hour." This is a lifetime curriculum.

Crucial Concerns for the Ordering and Transformation of Personality Disorders

The Concern for Assuming and Challenging the Core of Self-Centeredness in Each Human Being

The narcissistic personality disorder demonstrates that the core of self-centeredness is the controlling motif in some persons' lives. Yet Christian pietism's sweetness-and-light view of the individual and community life of Christians ignores, overlooks, and shows little concern for the wisdom of Paul when he says, "Therefore let any one who thinks he stands take heed lest he fall. No temptation has overtaken you that is not common to man" (1 Cor. 10:12–13). That means all of us. The temptation of self-centeredness is common to us all. The assumption of a core of self-centeredness is a working principle of psychiatry that makes of us individually and collectively what Scott Peck has called "the people of the lie." "The lie" is essentially what evil is. As Peck (1983:123–124) says, "The evil deny the suffering of their guilt—the painful awareness of their sin, inadequacy and imperfection—by casting their pain onto others through projection and scapegoating. They themselves may not suffer, but those around them do. They cause suffering. The evil create for those under their dominion a miniature sick society."

The admixture of evil in good is the nemesis of the spiritually naive. The assumption of the core of self-centeredness was explicit in Jesus' appreciation of the understanding of this "dark side" or shadow of our beings when he said to his disciples, "Behold, I send you out as sheep in the midst of wolves; so be wise as serpents and innocent as doves" (Matt. 10:16). To assume a core of self-centeredness in our own and others' beings is to be as "wise as serpents."

An Evenhanded Challenge of the Power-Success Syndrome

The foremost wisdom of the serpent is that the core of self-centeredness takes the form of the lust for power. In the temptation of Eve and Adam in the Garden of Eden, the serpent was not appealing to their physical hunger. He was appealing to their need to "be like God" (Gen. 3:5). Erich Fromm (1966:43) says this is idolatry, "the craving for possession, power, fame, and so forth."

The sanctification of the power-success syndrome is the beguiling temptation of the followers of Jesus Christ. When Jesus used the surgical metaphor of plucking out the offending eye or cutting off the offending hand, he used it to refer to *two* kinds of lust, the lust for sex (Matt. 5:29–30) and the lust for power—"Who is greatest in the kingdom of heaven?" (Matt. 18:7–9). The power struggles in the churches and denominations are saturated with the lust for power. This lust causes children and young persons in their tender years to stumble. This is the hallmark of the narcissistic and the sanctimonious antisocial or hostile-aggressive personality in the life of the churches.

We must evenhandedly challenge this lust in ourselves and those who would lord it over others. To do so requires both self-examination and courage to confront it in the deceptive gamesmanship of the power-hungry in the church. This is a part of the agenda for ordering our personal lives and the life of the community of faith. Underneath its manifestations in the churches and in the work force are homes where rejection and hostility have been the ruling motif in child-rearing. Family life education at the small-group level can point to a more excellent way in the challenge of the power politics of the family. The ministerial leadership of the churches can challenge power hunger by being an example to people instead of "lording it over them" (1 Peter 5:3; cf. Mark 10:42ff.). Lay leadership in the church can do the same. Many times lay leaders actually compete for the position of the pastor but would not want to live on the salary they would get if offered the job!

The Concern for the Grace of Teachableness

The sum total of the core of self-centeredness and the lust for power is hardness of heart—the unwillingness to listen to others or to learn from anyone. We have seen this as a common trait in all personality disorders. Down in the human heart this hardness is spawned in the defective upbringing of the person or in his or her despair at ever being able to measure up to the seemingly impossible ideal of the nevertheless loving and considerate parent. For example, the overgenerosity of affluent parents can undercut the initiative of the growing child and a passive-aggressive life-style can ensue. The child can take any gift except instruction and wisdom. Hardheadedness—a good American word for hardness of heart—is the result.

One opposite of hardness of heart is openness of heart, mind, and spirit. Another is tenderness of heart. I have chosen to blend openness and tenderness of heart into the embracing thought of teachableness. Jesus said that Moses gave married persons permission for divorce because of their hardness of heart. The *Good News Bible* translates: "Moses gave you permission to divorce your wives because you are so hard to teach" (Matt. 19:8). Usually this unteachableness takes the form of resistance or anger. The apostle Paul says in Ephesians 4:26, 32: "Be angry but do not sin . . . and be kind to one another, tenderhearted, forgiving one another, as God in Christ forgave you." Anger legitimately is a response to real or perceived hurt, frustration, and injustice. It only opens the personal encounter. To let the sun go down upon it and give way to it in unforgiveness is to harden the heart. To pursue it to reconciliation and forgiveness leads to tenderness of heart and to learning from the other person where we ourselves have erred. Thus a marriage conflict, a church quarrel, a struggle for power, or a clash of wills is a potential learning situation and not necessarily an evil in and of itself. Yet the commitment to learning what your or my opponent has to teach us is the rub. This makes the difference between personality disorder and order. Are we willing to make room in our hearts for the other person? As the apostle Paul appealed, "Open your hearts to us; we have wronged no one, we have corrupted no one, we have taken advantage of no one. I do not say this to condemn you, for I said before that you are in our hearts, to die together and to live together" (2 Cor. 7:2–3). This is a mutual process, and without mutuality of teachableness perplexity remains and despair can take over in a human relationship. It implies a mutual willingness to listen to the other, to attend to what he or she is saying or doing and what this *means.* This covenant of teachableness and open-hearted listening is an indispensable part of the church fellowship's agenda for dealing with personality disorder and bringing order out of the chaos of human relationships through a fellowship of love according to knowledge.

This cannot be done in our own strength. Our ingrained core of self-centeredness defeats that. The Spirit of the resurrected Christ alone enables us. That enabling took place for Cleopas and his friends after they walked and talked together with the Stranger on the road to Emmaus:

> When he was at table with them, he took the bread and blessed, and broke it, and gave it to them. And their eyes were opened and they recognized him; and he vanished out of their sight. They said to each other, "Did not our hearts burn within us while he talked to us on the road, while he opened to us the scriptures?" (Luke 24:30–32)

What an antithesis to the hard-bitten dogmatists who use the scriptures to beat other people into submission to their ambitions!

Probably the most widespread religious form of hardness of heart is unbending, unyielding, harsh religious dogmatism, especially when it is used in the family, the pulpit, and the personal religious conference to punish people. This dogmatism can be the kind of belittlement, disparagement, and verbal abuse we discussed as being a root cause of the avoidant personality disorder. When it is gullibly incorporated by a person it can be the religious form of the compulsive personality disorder. When rejected outright it can lay the groundwork for religious antisocial behavior. Hard hearts reproduce themselves.

The Concern for Self-Worth and the Ministry of Encouragement

It would seem that a concern for the self-worth of each person within the reach of the church's ministry of encouragement would be contradictory to a frank appraisal of the core of self-centeredness. To the contrary, the Christian sense of personal self-worth is objectively grounded in the image of God within us in which God created us. It springs from our having been bought with a price in that we are persons for whom Christ died. Yet this same Christ enables us subjectively to realize our self-worth in that he does not ask of us that we overidealize him. He suffered temptation as we do, he took upon himself the same limitations we have, he is moved with compassion toward us in our self-rejection, and he believes in and loves us when we do not believe in and love ourselves. When we give in to temptation, he assures us as he did Simon Peter that we can still turn around and become a strength and encouragement to our fellow strugglers. We can come to him with boldness to find help in time of need. In his command that we always be reaching for maturity and wholeness, he does not require that we deny either our or his humanity.

Hence, Christ pours the treasure of his ministry of encouragement into the earthen vessels of our selfhood. He enables us to invest confidence in other people's possibilities as they take practical steps to bring these workable gifts into reality. The mission of the church in nurturing the flowering of self-worth into a clear purpose in life offsets the low sense of self-esteem that specifically underlies the dependent, the passive-aggressive, the asocial, and the avoidant personality disorders and that underlies the rest of them more generally.

Nurturing and Appreciating the Meditative and Contemplative Life of Prayer

One of the spiritual nutriments missing in much of the activistic and aggressive life of many Christian groups is the solid appreciation of the less "social" persons such as those with the asocial, the avoidant, and even the paranoid personality disorders. In order to form a relationship to these persons a congregation and its ministers can slow their pace, take more time than would be required for "instant" friendships to form, and learn to appreciate the distance and solitude that shy, reclusive people seem to require. We can draw strength and specific skills in this from Thomas Merton and Morton Kelsey in the Catholic tradition; Rufus Jones, Thomas Kelly, and Douglas Steere in the Quaker tradition; and Howard Thurman and Edward Thornton in the Methodist and Baptist traditions. As I have said before, such contemplativeness and meditation on our part slows us down enough so that we are enabled to "connect" with the shy, the boring, the recluse, the eccentric, and even the paranoid individuals. They may choose to remain as anonymous church participants. They may never come to church but surreptitiously give money, do good deeds, call us by telephone most unexpectedly, or come to see us when they hear we are in trouble. The main thing is that there is a core of warmth at the center of their being if we have the patience, steadfastness, and contemplativeness to connect with it and to know it when we see it. It is ever so subtle!

The Priority of Steadfastness and Durability in Relationships with Individuals and Families

A common denominator in all those afflicted with personality disorders is the impaired ability of these persons to form and maintain durable relationships. In friendships, in marriage, and in work their life-styles are all characterized by brevity, brokenness, and alienation of relationships. As a result of isolation, loneliness, divorce, and difficulty in keeping a job they are thrust into a personality, economic, and cultural slide throughout the course of their lives. Their religious lives suffer a similar fate. They become religious itinerants as they break relationships with or are rejected by one fellowship after another. More often there is no dramatic break. The church and its ministers simply lose touch with them. They drop through the cracks of the religious community as well as of the mental health community.

Yet in the love of Jesus Christ we have a love that will not let us go. The essential message of the resurrection of Jesus Christ is that in him we have a relationship that even death itself cannot break, but only change. The steadfastness and immovableness of one human being's basic concern and de- votion to the person who does everything in the book to invite despair, rejection, and hostility is at first surprising good news. Then it is so unreal as to be subjected to further tests. Finally, having survived all, it stands. This testing calls for candor, frank setting of limits, genuine humor, and confes- sion of real mistakes when they are made. Thus even the borderline, stably unstable person begins to experience some integrity and reliability in the world. In relating to persons with pronounced personality disorders, you and I must "sit easy in the saddle, for it is a long journey," as a veteran pastor told me as he witnessed me doing my first pastoral work as if it all had to be accomplished in one summer.

The concern for steadfastness in personal relationships is the primary and consummate issue on the agenda of the church and its ministry as a community of the hope of the resurrection. The need for this is the pressing challenge of the care of persons with manifest personality disorders. Breakage of relationships is their shared tragedy. The small- group life of the church has much to offer in offsetting this tragedy. Skilled marriage and family therapy by both lay and professional people can be helpful too. Yet the consciousness of both religious and mental health personnel of the need for *continuity* of relationships for their constituency is at a low level. For example, the *personal* pastor, the *personal* physician, and the *personal* physician-psychiatrist are endangered species in today's religious and medical systems. Yet the nature of the Christian faith and the medical care of the whole person de- mand such continuity of care.

We have come to the end of our conversation about un- masking personality disorders in maladapted persons. Their difficulties in living are *social* difficulties. Their problems in becoming lastingly related to spouses, children, schools, jobs, and the Christian community point almost as often to the shallowness and defectiveness of our cultural values, beliefs, and expectations as to the intensive interactions between par- ents and children. Again and again we have seen their broken- ness as microcosms of the brokenness of our American culture. We have seen religious behaviors that reflect rather than prophetically challenge the brokenness of our American culture. We are faced with the challenge: "By the crowd have they been broken, by the crowd they shall be healed." In the resurrected community of those who have been crucified with Christ, we live, yet not we, but Christ lives in us, and we are called indeed to live a life ordered by him. In the life of that community we are persuaded that persons with disordered ways of existing no longer need the masks of sanity these disorders represent. Masks are so fatiguing. We can have done with them and be ministers of encouragement to enable others to do likewise.

Bibliography

American Psychiatric Association. 1980. *Diagnostic and Statistical Manual of Mental Disorders* (DSM III). Washington, D.C.: American Psychiatric Association.

Augsburger, David W. 1986. *Pastoral Counseling Across Cultures.* Philadelphia: Westminster Press.

Benson, Herbert. 1975. *The Relaxation Response.* New York: William Morrow & Co.

Berne, Eric. 1972. *What Do You Say After You Say Hello? The Psychology of Human Destiny.* New York: Grove Press.

Bowlby, John. 1973. *Separation: Anxiety and Anger.* New York: Basic Books.

———. 1979. *The Making and Breaking of Affectional Bonds.* New York: Methuen.

———. 1982. *Loss: Sadness and Depression.* New York: Basic Books.

———. 1983. *Attachment.* 2nd ed. New York: Basic Books.

Bunyan, John. [1678] 1903. *The Pilgrim's Progress.* New York: Fleming H. Revell Co.

Cleckley, Hervey. 1955. *The Mask of Sanity.* St. Louis: C. V. Mosby Co.

Coles, Robert. 1978. *Festering Sweetness: Poems of American People.* Pittsburgh: University of Pittsburgh Press.

Colson, Charles W. 1976. *Born Again.* Old Tappan, N.J.: Fleming H. Revell Co.

Courier-Journal, Louisville, Ky., September 17, 1986, p. A-13.

Cranfield, Charles E. B. 1979. *A Critical and Exegetical Commentary on the Epistle to the Romans.* 6th ed. Vol. 2. International Critical Commentary. Edinburgh: T.& T. Clark.

DSM III. *See* American Psychiatric Association.

Elkind, David. 1981. *The Hurried Child: Growing Up Too Fast Too Soon.* Reading, Mass.: Addison-Wesley Publishing Co.

Erikson, Erik H. 1964. *Insight and Responsibility.* New York: W. W. Norton & Co.

———. 1968. *Identity: Youth and Crisis.* New York: W. W. Norton & Co.

————. 1977. *Toys and Reasons: Stages in the Ritualization of Experience.* New York: W. W. Norton & Co.

Freud, Sigmund. [1914] 1951. "On Narcissism: An Introduction." *The Complete Psychological Works of Sigmund Freud.* Vol. 4. London: Hogarth Press.

Friedman, Meyer, and Ray H. Rosenman. 1974. *Type A Behavior and Your Heart.* New York: Alfred A. Knopf.

Fromm, Erich. 1947. *Man for Himself: An Enquiry Into the Psychology of Ethics.* New York: Rinehart & Co.

————. 1966. *You Shall Be as Gods: A Radical Interpretation of the Old Testament and Its Tradition.* New York: Holt, Rinehart & Winston.

————. 1973. *The Anatomy of Human Destructiveness.* New ed. New York: Holt, Rinehart & Winston.

Gabbard, Glen O. 1985. "The Role of Compulsiveness in Physics." *Journal of the American Medical Association* 254(20) 2926–2929.

Hiltner, Seward. 1952. *The Counselor in Counseling.* Nashville: Abingdon-Cokesbury Press.

Hinsie, L. E., and R. J. Campbell, eds. 1970. *Psychiatric Dictionary.* 4th ed. New York: Oxford University Press.

Hoffer, Eric. 1951. *The True Believer: Thoughts on the Nature of Mass Movements.* New York: Harper & Row.

Kierkegaard, Søren. [1849] 1941. *The Sickness Unto Death.* Tr. by Walter Lowrie. Princeton: Princeton University Press.

————. [1843] 1944. *Either/Or.* Tr. by Walter Lowrie. Vol. 2. Princeton: Princeton University Press.

————. [1847] 1946. *Works of Love.* Tr. by David F. Swenson and Lillian Marvin Swenson. Princeton: Princeton University Press.

Lester, Andrew D. 1983. *Coping with Your Anger: A Christian Guide.* Philadelphia: Westminster Press.

Loder, James E. 1981. *The Transforming Moment: Understanding Convictional Experience.* New York: Harper & Row.

Luther, Martin. [1517] 1957. *Luther's Ninety-five Theses.* Tr. by C. M. Jacobs. Philadelphia: Fortress Press.

Madden, Myron. 1970. *The Power to Bless.* Nashville: Broadman Press.

Millon, Theodore. 1981. *Disorders of Personality: DSM III; Axis II.* New York: John Wiley & Sons.

Oates, Wayne E. 1971. *Confessions of a Workaholic.* Nashville: Abingdon Press.

————. 1985. *Managing Your Stress.* Philadelphia: Fortress Press.

Peck, M. Scott. 1983. *The People of the Lie: The Hope for Healing Human Evil.* New York: Simon & Schuster.

Reich, Charles A. 1970. *The Greening of America: How the Youth Revolution Is Trying to Make America Livable.* New York: Random House.

Reid, William H. 1983. *Treatment of the DSM-III Psychiatric Disorders.* New York: Brunner/Mazel.

Reiser, David E., and Hanna Levenson. 1984. "Abuses of the Borderline Diagnosis." *American Journal of Psychiatry* 141(12):1528.

Relman, Arnold S. 1980. "The New Medical-Industrial Complex." *New England Journal of Medicine* 303:963–970.

Robertson, Archibald, and Alfred Plummer. [1914] 1953. *A Critical and Exegetical Commentary on the First Epistle of St. Paul to the Corinthians.* 2nd ed. Edinburgh: T. & T. Clark.

Rogers, Carl R. 1951. *Client-Centered Therapy: Its Current Practice, Implications, and Theory.* Boston: Houghton Mifflin Co.

Samuelson, Robert J. 1986. "How Companies Grow Stale." *Newsweek,* September 8, 1986.

Selye, Hans. 1976. *The Stress of Life.* Rev. ed. New York: McGraw-Hill Book Co.

Sullivan, Harry Stack. 1947. *Conceptions of Modern Psychiatry.* Washington, D.C.: William Alanson White Psychiatric Foundation.

———. 1953. *The Interpersonal Theory of Psychiatry.* New York: W. W. Norton & Co.

Tiebout, Harry M. 1950. "The Act of Surrender in the Treatment of Alcoholism." *Pastoral Psychology* 1(2):1.

Zee, Hugo G. 1980. "The Guyana Incident." *Bulletin of the Menninger Clinic* 44(4):345–363.